The Pagan Dream Guide

Dreamtime images symbolism and ancient wisdom

By

Pat Regan

Published 2021 by Can Write Will Write

http://www.canwritewillwrite.com

Copyright © Pat Regan 2021
Pat Regan asserts the moral right to be identified as the author of this work.
A catalogue record for this book is available in the British Library

ISBN-13: 978-1-78808-365-2

About the Author

Pat Regan was born and raised in Southport, Lancashire. He is a professional author, environmental campaigner and dedicated, life-long angler. A countryman of various talents, Pat was previously a tree surgeon and later become a surgical chiropodist, reflexologist, and sports massage therapist. He also helps his wife Cath manage a busy, preschool childcare facility.

Pat is the father of four children, and he is also well-known in Ufology and Paranormal circles.

Introduction

Many people may understandably see the vision in dreams of a savage tiger shark gripping their leg as a horrifying image. Just the sort of thing to wake one up late at night in a hot, heart-pounding sweat. On the other hand, it would perhaps seem difficult for most folk to view the image of a beautiful blue butterfly with anything other than timeless delight and awe. In the dreamworld anything is possible, but things may not always be as they initially seem!

The following list is of course not all-inclusive, no list ever can be. It must only be used as a general guide to enable the seeker of truth to enhance their psychic ability to reach deeper regions of the mind. The dreamer is usually the best person to interpret the dream. However, a better understanding of symbolism can help a great deal.

This succinct inventory of dreamtime imagery will hopefully prove to be useful to all seekers of greater wisdom, especially those wishing to partake in the ancient arts of divination.

This is not an egotistical claim by the author, for the divinity of the gods works through all things. We contain within our beings, real concrete aspects of divinity. The gods are of us, we are of the gods! The relationship is a symbiotic, two-way affair. It is as simple as that!

The sacred aspect resides within all who sincerely care to look for it. Dreams and symbolic images may be linked to events of past, present or future. The honest seeker in his/her interpretation of dreams must keep this fact in mind, always.

The following list although fleeting, may prove a good place to start upon this genuine quest for greater wisdom.

Dreamtime Imagery – The List

NB. Please note that the esoteric words 'magick' and 'magickal' are used in this book to differentiate from the stage magician's 'magic'.

ABYSS: The underworld, the unknown. The depths of the subconscious mind. Fear of strange things that cannot be seen or understood.

ACROBAT: The symbol of reversal, seeing people or events from another point of perspective/view. Tarot image of the Hanged Man links with acrobat (reversed man), thus leading to self-sacrificial imagery.

ACCIDENT: Blatant (cops and robber) movie/television images of course flood through the popular consciousness every night. May however relate to prior warnings over future short-term travel. Alternatively, might be a warning against taking unwise actions in business enterprises, love affairs, etc.

ADMINISTRATOR: Figure of authority with capacity to harm oneself and one's family. If the figure is masculine, then may relate to one's father/schoolteacher. If female, then the domineering mother. The need for liberation from suppression. Warning to discover who or what is giving you a hard time.

AEROPLANE: The astral plane, higher levels of consciousness. Escape from problems or worries. Freedom from dictatorships also, because of cross shape, sacrifice (esp. true for Christian-interpreters) and the four elements, earth, air, fire, and water.

AFFAIR (love): State of wishing for greener grass on the other side of the fence. Desire to improve one's sexual/emotional connections with others. The need for attention and to be loved. Warning not to lead your life on emotional levels only.

AILMENTS: This may herald a situation/occurrence that will lead to trouble or unfavourable result. My also relate to damaged ego following emotional setback. Sometimes means that events will be delayed.

ALCOHOL: The desire to escape from everyday problems and responsibilities. Also, if drinking in company, the need for stimulating companionship or acceptance. May foretell celebrations, weddings etc, to come.

ALTAR: Place of spiritual authority. Gateway to other dimensions/levels of existence. In simpler terms; place of judgement, liberation, and self-sacrifice.

AMETHYST: Mental stability and good fortune to come. Satisfaction in all matters of the mind.

AMMUNITION: To a woman, seeing ammunition is to behold the seed produced and fired by the phallic member (which is the gun/bow/weapon of masculinity). To a man, ammo is the fertilising spermatozoon. If ammo lies untouched, then can be sign of sterility or sexual frustration. If being fired, then depicts the need for sexual satisfaction.

Animals

An exceptionally large subject this one. We shall look at several prime examples here, remembering that interpretations may be most variable and dependent on individual outlook.

ALLIGATOR: symbol of the terrors or the unknown; the deep uncharted depths of the reptilian lower mind. A warning to take care. Also, to be aware of deceptive friends or cunning authorities purporting to have your best concerns at heart.

ANTS: Sign of minor troubles worrying the interpreter. Any such creatures that get under one's feet in annoying fashion are firm warnings to stop letting insignificant matters clog up one's life.

APE: Sign of betrayal and deceit. Beware, someone is not being straight with you. Watch your back or you will be taken for a ride.

BAT: Bats are symbolic of the unconscious; they belong to the realm of darkness and thus the unknown or feared aspects of self. Often seen as an emblem of death/illness. Much of the bat's bad press is through the negative efforts of the early church to conjoin it with evil and the Devil. A great shame because they are quite charming little fellows really! The Chinese regard bats as a sign of happiness and contentment; quite a contrast to western negative thoughts on this creature.

BEAR: Symbol of crude unpredictable power and stress. The rampant egotistical side of self that must be sometimes put in its place. Also, the primordial giant, the oppressor, or the school bully.

BEAVER: Sign of striving hard towards one's ambition without much rest. Also, may be seen as a symbol of overcoming problems that seem larger than oneself.

Although usually a peaceful animal, beavers are strong and certainly not afraid to attack big carnivores that try to eat them. Therefore, symbolic of resistance against oppression.

BEE: Organisation; industrious action; advancement and creative productivity. This is a very ancient Pagan emblem of working towards one's required aspirations. A good sign of successful struggles and teamwork towards a common aim.

BOAR: Because of its 'head down and charge' mentality, the boar stands as a sign of wild, unthinking bravado. To see it in dreams is a warning to look before you leap. You may be about to embark upon an imprudent course of events in your life, so check out your plans from all angles before it is too late!

BULL: The horns of the bull are a strong lunar symbol. Many cultures held this animal in high esteem as a sign of various atmospheric deities. To some it was lunar, others had it as a mark of the Thunder god, whilst to the Romans it was the Sun bull of the solar/war god Mithras. It represents the (masculine) fertilising shafts of sunlight that bring new life to the waiting (feminine) earth. It is suggestive of strong male sexuality or frequently libido that can become obsessively all-embracing, i.e., rage. Thus, the bull is quite a complex emblem, much more than just a 'bull in a China shop'.

CAMEL: This odd creature is emblematic of the conscious mind. This is because the camel is a beast of the hot regions blessed (and sometimes cursed) by the Sun. The Sun is of the conscious light of day aspect, whereas the Moon depicts the deeper subconscious levels of night. The camel is a good sign, it is the animal that represents hope and survival in hostile environments.

CAT: Cats in dreams are frequently warnings of dangers to come. They, because of their magickal associations are symbolic of the instinctive self. Black cats are often linked to the negative, rather than positive aspects of life such as death and destruction. Many cats together are a warning to beware of attacks from enemies. Being scratched by a seemingly friendly cat in a dream foreshadows deceitful actions against you by family or acquaintances. The sound of a cat mewing denotes people you trust telling falsehoods behind your back, time to beware! The cat is the creature that links us to silent levels of deep self. Without doubt dangers may come with the sign of the cat but wisdom is also closely related to this animal. To see it as a purely negative emblem is imprudent.

CHAMELEON: The creature of change. Their well-known trait of altering their skin colour to match backgrounds gives us a strong clue to just why/how the sub-conscious mind uses them in symbolic communication. They stand as emblems of deceit and mistrust. What cannot be seen, perceived, or understood is usually not something in that the layman believes he can trust. The chameleon is then the quintessential warning of the turncoat in our midst. We should view it as a sign that all is not as it first appears!

CHICKENS: Frequently seen as a sign of minor troubles. Although chickens are winged creatures they have (because of their reluctance to fly) strong associations with the earth element. Their persistent habit of scratching the ground for food is analogically connected to annoying little problems that plague the mind and stop us being at one with our self.

COW: Sign of the winter turning into the warm abundance of summer. Also, a symbol of kind, maternal instincts, and care. The cow has lunar, air, and earth associations. The Egyptian goddess Hathor was frequently portrayed in the guise of a cow. The great Isis also frequently sported cow's horns upon her head although this link probably owes much to her amalgamation with Hathor. This gentle creature was oft revered then as a spiritual sign of the great mother goddess of the universe. This is a far cry from today as the cow is now treated as nothing more than a milk machine, to be exploited for profit. She is artificially inseminated, robbed of her calf when it is but days old and finally killed young as a worn-out milker to make unhealthy burgers etc. Many then will associate this sign with pregnancy and maternal instinct. However, to a dedicated vegan (one who abstains from consuming animal products including eggs and milk), the cow stands as a prime totem of man's vagarious greed and destruction against Mother Earth.

CROCODILE: To see the vision of this creature is to be warned in a very sure manner indeed. Do not trust anyone who appears to relate to this image for to do so is to court bad fortune and disaster. Animals that crawl out of dark waters in a dangerous fashion represent the negative aspects of self, secretly lurking in the hidden pools of the deep, subconscious mind.

DOG: Multi-complex symbol. Happy dogs denote loyalty and friendships. Fighting, snarling dogs warn of enemies in our midst. Legendary black dogs have often appeared throughout history to warn people before disaster occurs. The awesome, mythical three-headed dog, Cerberus is the guardian of Pluto's kingdom. He reminds us of the dog's role as faithful servant unto death. Cerberus, with his triple-head aspect, becomes a type of dreaded holy trinity. He is friend ally and especially conservator to the righteous. Alternatively, he is monster, fiend, and devourer to the wicked. Baying, lonely dogs herald (like the Banshee) death, sadness, and separation. Although, as we have seen, the dog is frequently associated with death its vital symbolism is essentially good/positive. The author often has visitations in dreamtime from his loyal black dog 'Midge' who left the physical dimension for pastures new some time ago. Midge usually gives warning that danger or error is close at hand. He also helps to find lost items. The dog then is never to be underestimated. His (or her) intimate connection and loyalty to mankind stretches far back into the mists of pre-history. His staunch faithfulness to us bridges many barriers, even

14

death itself. The wise will accept this image as a true gift from the old gods; these images are I often believe the visiting spirits of our loyal canine pals (that are not really lost at all.) Ignore them at your peril!

DONKEY: Mules, Donkeys and Asses are, because of their sometimes-contentious nature, the rank embodiment of symbolised stubbornness. As a beast of burden, this animal represents slow but sure progress with delays along the way. Loud aggressive braying is a mark of the fool, laughing behind your back. To dream of one is a sign that the individual should look to higher things instead of getting bogged down with business affairs and the like. Time for a holiday perhaps?

ELEPHANT: Sign of great wealth and good fortune. To ride an elephant is to rise highly above lesser mortals. Even the tiger trembles before man on this lofty plateau. If this symbol appears before us in any form, then business, financial, matrimonial, and other affairs ahead may bode well.

FOX: The old cartoon stereotypes of the sly old fox is not far from the truth. He denotes deceit, theft, risk, and malpractice. The fox was frequently seen throughout mediaeval Christian Europe as a sign of Satan. Although Pagans do not believe in a devil figure, the negative concepts of this symbol should be heeded well. Nevertheless – also a totem symbol of great resourcefulness.

FROG: A sign of childhood and the summer. Also emblematic of transformation. The old fairy tale of the frog changing into the handsome prince is ancient evidence of the animal's shape shifting abilities. What child has not looked on in awe as the spawn converts into a tadpole, which in turn transforms into the frog? The frog marks the transition of elements, especially water into earth. It reminds us of our own evolution from the first primordial seas and our inescapable link to the waters of our mother's womb. To generalise, this is a positive symbol that represents our evolving pathway through life. The situation of the frog in dreams (i.e., good, or bad) tells the interpreter whether events are boding favourably or otherwise for the future.

GAZELLE: This lovely little creature has the symbolic honour of usually being portrayed in the role of victim. This isn't at all surprising when we remember that gazelles form a substantial part in the diet of large carnivores such as lions. To see a gazelle on astral levels can be a warning to beware. You may become a victim yourself if you are not careful. Also, a sign to be wary of persecution from enemies that lurk close by. The old maxim 'Look before you leap' rings true in this case. Its habit of jumping has been compared by some to the soul's quest for perfection on the swings, slides, and roundabouts of the eternal cosmic dance that we call life.

GIRAFFE: Symbol of attaining goals that seem to be out of reach. Going beyond the normal to achieve the desires that have eluded one for a long time.

GOAT: Because of over a thousand years of monotheistic misrepresentation, the goat has been cast as a sign of evil. The Church, in its relentless hysterical mania in fact converted most horned animals into wicked agents of the Prince of Darkness himself. This creature is symbolic of masculine, fertilising (god force) aspects in nature that are crucial for new life and evolution. To see it in dreamtime often relates to the individual's own libido. The image of Old Horny is an immensely powerful sign of the archaic Horned god of all nature. His name changes throughout history and within divergent cultural systems however his rural, green lustiness reminds us that without this holy primitive force we would soon become (like the dinosaurs) totally sterile and ultimately quite extinct!

HARE: Queen Boudicca released a hare from the folds of her cloak both as a rite for spiritual conciliation and for divination before engaging Roman forces in battle. Hares have been regarded as a sacred shape-shifting animal since very ancient times. On the subconscious level, it denotes stamina with ability to avoid obstacles. It also signifies indecisiveness because of its tendency to quickly switch direction when evading predators. The ancients regarded hares as a lunar animal sacred to the Moon goddess. The Chinese saw it as being essentially feminine connected with the Yin principal of creation. Because of this we may link it to the anima (feminine/goddess aspect) when it is seen in a man's dream. Breaking away for a moment from natural Pagan symbolism of the hare, we can observe an old link to monotheistic female suppression here if we examine the Hebrew representation of this creature. To them it symbolised, because of its feminine aspect, lust, and wanton fecundity. The Old Testament describes hares as being 'unclean'. This term was often used to denigrate menstruating women into second-class citizens, thereby leaving spiritual monopoly firmly in the grip of masculine hands. In old farming communities the last sheath of corn to be cut in a field was believed to contain the inherent corn spirit. This spiritual entity was frequently depicted as an animal, moreover it was often given to be seen in the form of a hare. Could the word 'Harvest' originate from an older more colloquial phrase 'hare-vest/hare-feast/hare-festival'? It doesn't seem too farfetched at all does it?

HORSE: This is another multi-complex symbol. Horses are sacred to numerous deities. The waves of the sea are attributed to the Greek Poseidon/the Celtic Manannan and (or) the Roman Neptune. The god Mars had horse races held in his honour during the months of March and October. The sudden unexpected appearance of a horse was deemed to be an ill omen of death and destruction. Odin/Woden rode an eight-legged Horse (Sleipnir) through the sky. This symbol is strongly associated with man's animal nature and survival instincts. Seeing yourself in control of a wild horse is to master these lower, sometimes negative aspects of self that

17

can billow up and threaten the higher intellectual capacity. A wild uncontrollable steed running joyfully is the ultimate symbol of freedom and liberation. How it relates to the individual and their lifestyle is a matter for serious thought. At the risk of generalisation, the horse can be regarded as a beneficent, yet most dynamic of emblems.

HYENA: If one is down on one's luck and life is giving back nothing but sadness and sorrow, then symbols like the hyena are frequently experienced. This can also be a warning sign that somebody or something is plotting against you. Time to watch your back and count your friends, with special care!

JACKAL: The symbolism of this canine scavenger follows a similar form to that of the Hyena. The gods in their wisdom will often bring the vision of the lowly scavenging creatures of the earth to mind when enemies plot against us. Alternately though, the scavenger is vital to the wellbeing of the planet. We must remember that such animals literally 'pick up the pieces.' Because of this, fact jackals frequently appears after we have experienced great sadness in life. The saturnine time when we must pick up the pieces and move on to greener pastures anew.

KANGAROO: This strange, ungainly marsupial comes to us as a sign of transformation. The young Joey snuggles warmly inside mum's pouch. The adults suddenly spring off at great speed without warning, changing direction with gazelle-like ease. The animal can also lash out its hind legs with immense power to inflict harm on pursuers. All these attributes and more put the kangaroo into a symbolic category which is not that dissimilar to another creature of transformation, the hare! To see a kangaroo in dreams/visions is a sign that one will achieve success by outwitting jealous rivals or foes.

LAMB: To parents, the lamb is subconsciously linked to their children. "My little lamb!" and similar sentiments illustrate this point quite clearly. The lamb is the sign of innocence, so any vision, which involves cruelty to them, denotes harm coming to the observer or their own offspring. Much of the lamb's earlier connection with sacrifice can be traced to the grossly sickening laws on burnt offerings, found in the book of Leviticus in the Bible. It is strange that even today such an innocent creature should still be treated so badly. The vile horrors of intensive factory farming will unfortunately ensure that the lamb continues to suffer needlessly, for the desires of mankind. To the modern omnivore/carnivore then, the lamb is a somewhat awkward and uncomfortable symbol to come to terms with. To devour innocence is to gorge on one's own offspring, albeit in abstract fashion. Subconsciously, it may occasionally be likened to incest. I wonder how many people have (like the late well-known vegetarian writer/cook Linda McCartney) omitted meat from their diet after watching lambs at play; whilst at the same time questioning the reddened contents of their dinner plate? The power of symbolism to change lives is very great indeed. The seemingly insignificant lamb is no exception to this magickal truth.

LLAMA: Somewhat like a cross betwixt a horse and a camel, with the camel part gaining in prominence. Its slow beast of burden characteristics gives this animal symbolic ties with creatures like the mule and the ass. View the llama as a steady sign of durability in life's adverse conditions.

LEOPARD: The leopard cannot change his spots and as such this animal is a sign that danger lurks in the most unlikely of situations. The unseen stalker in usually the one that gets you so to see the Leopard on higher levels is a sure warning from the old ones to beware of menace posing as serene beauty. The savage spirit cat draws its life breath from our deepest fears!

LION: Lions are symbolic of achieving great goals; moreover, they are sacred to many solar gods/goddesses. They signify awesome power in nature/man. Because of their all-consuming/devouring aspect they also represent the eternal qualities of time itself. The lion stands as probably the most potent vision of victory and valour known to mankind. This aspect of victory is certainly not only to be perceived in a militaristic sense. The Egyptian goddess Tefnut was often depicted as a Lioness; she was the presiding deity of moisture. Without water there is of course no life so in this context we see the lion gaining victory over the realm of drought and ultimately death itself.

LIZARD: Very much a symbol of minor irritations. The lizard is a smaller version of the snake and this in turn leads us to that mythical totem of life force, the dragon. Because of their quick alarming actions, they also denote unexpected accidents and misadventures.

LOBSTER: Anything with sharp claws that crawls out of the water should be viewed with caution. Water, especially deep-sea water is inherently linked to the subconscious mind. The lobster, because of its rich food association, can however be a beneficent sign. Also, because of the way that lobsters change colour after being boiled, they are symbolic of transformation. A lot depends on how close one's life revolves around such a symbol. A trawlerman's vision of a lobster will be vastly divergent from an office worker's view of the same thing.

MICE: The sign that domestic/family affairs are getting too much for you. Time to take a break away from the humdrum everyday aspects of life.

MOLE: Because of the way moles burrow about unseen by human eyes, they are analogous with hidden worries. Anything that blindly tunnels along like the mole is symbolic of arguments and strife for to go ahead without direction is to invite certain trouble and misfortune.

MONGOOSE: This animal is well known for its snake-killing abilities. The snake is symbolic of earth energy thus we may perceive the mongoose as its master. It ranks as a powerful emblem of overcoming great, seemingly impossible adversities.

MONKEY: Many species of monkey are tainted with the image of 'snatch, grab and run!' This in nature is of course a quite natural survival instinct, yet in modern human society it is wholly taboo. The monkey then in dreams is the thief and rascal. To see him thus is a warning to beware of theft and to 'keep your hand on your ha'penny!'

OCTOPUS: This creature of the deep has eight tentacles, because of this it has associations with the Spider. Herein aspects of entrapment are then obvious. The figure eight is symbolic of balance (two circles joined.) The octopus and squid gave numerous nightmares to sailors of old. Something that rises up out of dark waters (i.e., the subconscious mind) has to be seen as a threat. This is especially so if the thing in question possesses eight large tentacles to grab you with. See it then as a warning of dangerous events to come.

OTTER: Otters represent dexterity and wisdom. The way they lie on their backs to crack open shellfish is comparable with man surmounting uncomfortable problems. Their habit of dipping then rising in tranquil streams is symbolic of the human quest for knowledge. An altogether pleasing totem of satisfactory events to come!

OX: Similar associations with other horned animals like the bull, goat, and the ram. An ancient agricultural sign of continuity and evolutionary progress on any level.

PANTHER: Sign of unseen forces working against the observer. Unexpected events occurring out of the blue. Imminent danger- beware!

PIG: An animal of the good earth. The old country maxim 'happy as Pigs in muck' gives us a clue to the role that this beast plays in symbolic interpretation. The mere thought of pigs happily grovelling about in filthy mud has a comical air to it. The author is chuckling right now with this odd vision in mind. Pigs then are a benevolent, slightly jovial sign of pleasant events to come.

PORCUPINE: Although not an altogether negative symbol, the porcupine is a sign of reluctance. Nobody in their right mind wants to get too close to those nasty sharp quills. Also, a symbol of self-defence and steady defiance against greater odds.

PRAIRIE DOG: Their fast responsive actions say it all. This animal is a sign of the alert mindset and everything that links with the mundane consciousness. To see it in dreamtime is a warning to beware of unexpected assaults from hidden foes.

RACCOON: Very much (like the monkey) a sign of theft. Also, symbolic of betrayal thus if you see this in visions you should examine with care your relationships with others. Things may not be quite as rosy as they at first appear!

RAT: The rat is not a favourable sign to behold. It denotes illness, injury, and deception. It stands as an emblem to warn us that life's little problems are becoming too much to deal with. Like the mouse, this sign urges us to take a break and leave the 'rat race' behind.

REINDEER: Symbolic of winter's months and Yuletide. Can also be seen as a sign of hardships being conquered by perseverance. Stick to your plans and do not let others dissuade you from your goals.

SCORPION: This sign strangely has sexual connotations. The sting in the tail aspect is generally considered to be quite phallic and emblematic of the act of male ejaculation. Also, a sign of death. Life and death are but different sides to the same coin. It is not surprising that symbols such as this exhibit both aspects of the natural cycle in one physical form.

SEAL: A creature that dwells in two elements, both the water and the earth. Because of its ungainly land movement's yet graceful marine capacity, this animal is symbolic of endeavouring to better one's position in life.

SNAKE: A most ambiguous totem sign if ever there was one. One of the most ancient symbols of the serpent is to be seen on the Caduceus, the Staff of Hermes. This emblem contains two serpents twined round a winged staff/wand. The twin snakes in this context denote the dual male/female creative forces of the cosmos. Because of this fact snakes represent both equilibrium and good health. Biblical association with the snake/evil was adopted much later. The serpent in the Garden of Eden being Lileth (Adam's first wife according to early Hebrew texts) come to tempt Eve. Pagan philosophy holds that the gods created all life forms, so each divergent species contains the negative/positive ability needed to survive. Christianity scapegoated the snake (and other unpopular species) to achieve its own missionary ends. Of course, the snake can kill – it must, to simply survive.

Yet think on dear reader, so does man and in a much greater, far more environmentally destructive fashion. This abused/misunderstood creature is then for modern man the sign of death and ill omen yet once it stood proud as a symbol of earth energy and the elements that give us the first breath of life. When the serpent bites its own tail, we see the completed circle of life and death and new life once again. Remember well the duality of the snake or be forever in fear of its venomous bite and dreaded sinister countenance.

SQUIRREL: Sign of the summer and good things therein. Squirrels are associated with trees and all things appertaining to them. They represent determined productivity and endurance.

STAG: The stag with its magickal connection to the great horned god Cernunnos needs no introduction. 'This fabulous creature leads Pwyll into the underworld and represents the power of magickal transformation.' I wrote these words in an earlier book published in1996 and they remain as an insight into this remarkable beast. Its antlers reach up high toward the heavens. They remind us of the twisted branches of trees; because of this the stag is intimately linked symbolically to the growing energies inherent in the natural cycle. The stag then is the magickal escort that transports us between the levels and heralds change in existence of both the spiritual and material realms.

TIGER: Symbolic of power, energy, superiority and sometimes cruelty. In eastern cultures it was linked to the new moon and the darker aspects of the human soul. Its lunar connection may be seen as the reverse of the lion's solar position. The beautiful striped skin of this beast denotes luxury and pleasure. The alternating dark/light pattern is suggestive of the principles of duality and equilibrium. Because of its complex nature it is not an easy sign to generalise on. In fact, no sign as we have observed before really is simple to decipher. Some however give us more clues than others about their symbolic meaning.

TOAD: Again, like the frog, this little creature is (because of its metamorphosis from tadpole) linked to the aspect of transformation. The connection is however traditionally given as a more negative one than that of the frog simply because of the toad's dry, warty appearance. Its darker seemingly sinister countenance and persistently unnerving stare gave rise to a mediaeval association with evil and the Devil. All these negative connections did the toad no favours at all. They are in fact charming, quite fascinating animals with an ability to magnetise humans for considerable lengths of time. Their sinister aspect links them to the night, water and most especially the Moon. They are emblematic of magick and the capacity to change direction at will.

TORTOISE: To see this animal's reflected image in waters or its appearance in rites of divination (such as the glowing embers of a fireplace) is a sign to slow down. It may also be viewed as a symbol of stagnation and lethargy. The gods will always show us what we need to know if we simply give them the space in our hearts to do so. The tortoise tells us that life is going at slow speed or alternatively that maybe it would be beneficial to take time out to have a well-earned rest!

WEASEL: Frequently a sign of deceit and dishonour yet may also mark the aspects of persistence and determination. The verdict for the weasel's symbolic meaning rests with other clues that may surround it in vision. We must observe what kinds of animal, people, situations etc are to be found in its company to discover the negative or indeed positive significance. This aspect of correlating symbols to other images that dwell close by can in fact apply to most all signs. To see the whole picture is the true mode to genuine divination. If you only look at one tree you will miss the rest of the forest's holistic beauty.

WHALE: Awesome symbol of what resides in the deepest parts of the human mind. Any vision that rises out of the mysterious dark waters of the sea (the subconscious) is to be taken seriously for here we find the essence of existence. The whale represents order in the vast uncharted waters of the mind. It may arrive as a timely warning of important events to come. Alternatively, it can herald fear of the unknown ahead that we do not wish to face. Fear itself is a prime motivator that enables us to go beyond the mundane consciousness and access levels of self previously not experienced.

ZEBRA: The old striped horse of the African veld is to be viewed in a similar context as the common horse. The Zebra though is to the horse what the wildcat is to the domestic tabby. This wilder cousin of the horse denotes unbridled energy. Its striped coat strengthens this point further because of its association with dual aspects of creation. Altogether an excellent symbol of progress that now ends our brief exploration of animal symbolism.

This brief examination of animal symbolism in dreams takes us back to the main list. Do please keep in mind that the best person to decipher a dream is the person that experiences it.

ANVIL: Sign of the Roman fire god Vulcan, and Hephaestus God of Blacksmiths who was later compounded with Vulcan. To see an anvil is a sign of new events to come that will be beneficial.

APPLE: Apples are a particularly good sign of riches and good fortune. They are also frequently seen as a herald of romance, love, and affection. The latter is especially so with rosy, red apples.

ARM: To see this symbol is a warning that one must sacrifice something dear to progress in one's mission. An arm that is cut off denotes financial or emotional loss. Mythologically speaking, an arm denotes strength and compromise as in tales of the Celtic God Nuada and the later Cornish Saint Mylor who adopted his ethos.

ARMCHAIR: Sign of the desire for peace and contentment. Also denotes family connections with older relatives for obvious reasons. May also represent lethargy and the ability to move on in life.

ARROW: If you are anxiously waiting news of an important event then the arrow is likely to appear before you just prior to its arrival. Check the surrounding symbols in your dream to discover if it warns of good or disappointing news.

ASTRA PROJECTION/ OUT OF BODY EXPERIENCE OR SOUL TRAVEL: Delusion, hallucination, and imagination – or something far greater, not yet fully understood? When is a dream something else entirely? Astral projection has been vigorously dismissed as a pseudoscience by contemporary boffins in white coats. The ladies and gentlemen who place all their faith in lumps of expensive machinery that go 'ping', will have no truck with any notion of soul travel as it does not fit in with their limited scientific agenda. They can find no evidence of it, so in their materialistic worldview it simply does not exist. Nevertheless, various concepts of astral projection/soul travel do exist in various spiritual traditions. In ancient Egypt, esoteric teachings presented the soul (ba) as having the ability to soar outside the physical body. The same or similar themes are recorded in many other archaic cultures. My own experiences with this phenomenon are as follows. However, to be frank, I include this data for interest purposes and care little if others believe me or not. As a child, I had several strange interludes regarding out of body experiences (OOBE). I would find myself flying high over the rooftops at night and looking down, whilst in an exhilarated state. I also had similar OOBE when in surgery during childhood, while having my tonsils removed. I recall being above the medics and look down on them, as they operated on me. More recently this year (2021) I had gone to sleep and woken up to find that I was touching a wall with my hands and fingers. I instinctively knew that I was floating, as I felt my feet lift high off the ground. With little effort I pushed myself through the air and across the room. It was great fun and performed with ease, although I felt somewhat wobbly and unbalanced at times. I purposely reiterated to myself that I was fully awake too and not fast asleep. I looked down and could see my wife. The feeling I experienced at this time was pure euphoria and just like it was when I was a child. I wanted this wonderful experience to go on forever, as it felt so amazingly liberating. Yes, clever scientists today (the ones that cannot cure the common cold) have all manner of complex answers for what had happened, relating to brain wave activity, etc. I am moreover quite aware of very lucid dreams too, but this was something extremely different and as authentic as everyday events. However, my belief is that my astral body or spirit had momentarily exited my physical body at these times. I was not dreaming but in a highly conscious state, high above my physical body that my spirit had just moved out of. I have never thought that the spirit is entirely restricted to only leave the physical body, at the time of death, so these amazing aerial experiences are not that strange to me. My life-long belief that we are spiritual beings residing within physical shells was confirmed by this latest OOBE. If the time after death is as euphoric as astral adventures, when the spirit decides to go walkabout, then I sincerely believe that the fun-filled, good times are yet to come. Fly on!

AUTUMN: The end of the season announces winter's hardship, yet it also marks the rich abundance of natural bounty. Because of this autumn can be either a positive or a negative sign.

AXE: Symbol of strength and dependability. Also, a sign of starting fresh projects that may prove advantageous to the seer. Change is approaching fast!

BABY: The situation that the aby is seen in reflects the message that needs to be understood. Sick babies denote hardships to be endured, while smiling happy tots tell us that life is soon to improve.

BARBER: To dream of such a person is a sign of business ventures, new opportunities, and change. Also, the desire to change oneself and escape any mundane situation one may be in.

BASEMENT: Seeing oneself in this place reflects what is resting in the subconscious mind. Other surrounding images in the basement must be heeded to ascertain the nature of the vision/dream. Can be a warning to listen to that little voice (the subconscious) that is trying hard to tell us something of vital importance.

BED: Much depends on what context the bed is seen in. For a young agile person, a sign of sexual progress or alternatively the need for rest from physical exertion. To the elderly, a sign again of rest and contentment or sometimes illness. On deeper levels, the Bed denotes the secure nature of a mother's womb and the solitude found therein.

BEETLES: Symbolic of minor irritations and family trouble. They have wings so also linked to escaping problems.

BEHEADING: Strong connections here with illness and depression. Also, a sign of 'losing one's head' in an emotional way after being let down by a lover or spouse. Plain warning to look out for trouble (a-head) very soon.

BELLS: May be heard in festive note or alternatively gloomy in nature. Happy sounding bells denote weddings and good news arriving soon. Tenebrific chimes herald loss, defeat, illness, and hardships (even funerals) on the horizon.

Birds

Like animals, this grouping is widely divergent. We shall simply brush over the more commonly known ones herein.

ALBATROSS: It was once believed that because these birds followed ships of old, they were the souls of lost sailors. Because of this association they are linked to reincarnation and the afterlife. Also, a sign of sea voyages to come.

BLUEBIRD: Sign of luxury, youth, and happy occasions.

CHAFFINCH: This bird may be common, yet its lovely song matched with its beautiful plumage is a joy to behold. A symbol of fine times and happy holidays.

COCKEREL: This chap is the quintessence of what his name logically implies i.e., cockiness. A symbol of proud arrogance and foolish over confidence if ever there was one. Warning to not rely solely on one's ego for progression through life.

CRANE: Symbolic of the desire for independence and liberty.

CROW: This bird has many links to the ancient Celtic goddess of battle and death, the Morrigan/Morrigu. This is not surprising when we remember that the Hoodie Crow would have enjoyed rich pickings on old battlefield sites, following the gross carnage. The crow's dark colour also links it with night and all things associated. A rather negative symbol then that warns one to be especially careful.

DABCHICK: This little bird denotes security and continuity. Anyone who has ever watched this amusing bird skulking about in the reeds will understand his persistent nature and realise how easily he relates to one's own situation. A good sign for sure.

DUCK: Of course, it is unwise to generalise on this family because of its vast diversity however ducks are commonly given to denote travel across water. They also represent finery and the need to impress acquaintances. Drab ducks stand for disappointment and low self-esteem. Ducks with beautifully coloured plumage are a sign of inflated egos and fat-cat luxury.

EAGLE: The bird of Jupiter (Iuppiter) King of the Roman gods. The grace and majestic power displayed by the eagle is emblematic of the spiritual principal and warm light of day.

It is the creature of the Sun and denotes understanding overcoming the dark powers of chaos. It is the ultimate symbol of victory and conquest over lower forces. It is not surprising then that the Roman legions held their eagle banners high in front of their advancing battalions, at every opportunity. In modern terms, to regularly see this sign tells one that events will be more favourable than expected.

FALCON: Sign of the hunter. To see a falcon is to take control of one's affairs and do great deeds, sometimes at the expense of others. Also symbolic of liberty and freedom.

FLAMINGO: This bird suggests safety in numbers. Also, the necessity to adopt and adapt a new routine for the benefit of one's own development on spiritual levels. The flamboyant plumage denotes prosperity.

GANNET: Sign of overindulgent greed. The way in which gannets launch their attacks on schools of small fish is emblematic of persecution and vilification. A symbol then to be aware of assaults from above. Maybe your career or business is not quite as secure as you thought it to be.

GULL: Another bird that depicts greed and selfishness. Also, because of its water association, a sign of sea voyage. To see a white gull soaring high against a blue sky represents the desire for freedom.

HAWK: Similar attributes to the falcon. Sometimes connects with feelings of cruelty to other people that stand in your way or work against you.

JACKDAW: If you see this bird in visions/dreams then beware of family arguments and disputes that may arise from seemingly small insignificant affairs. Also, like many other birds, the jackdaw because of its social nature has links with the aspect of safety in numbers. Its well-known scavenging habits suggests an association with frugality of emotion and the inability to share true feelings.

KESTRAL: This little bird of prey can be viewed in a similar fashion as other falcon/hawk type of hunters. Because of modern mans' intrusion into the countryside with new road schemes, this bird has quickly learnt the art of the scavenger. Kestrels, although primarily hunters, will (like the crow) add carrion to their diet if the opportunity arises. We can surmise then that this bird is gaining subconscious aspects, not dissimilar to the sinister ones held by crows. Thanks to man, the kestrel's contemporary role in symbolism is also now about to become one that contains darker aspects of transformation. Whether or not this is beneficial remains to be seen by future generations of seekers.

KINGFISHER: To see this bird is a blessing from the gods that lifts the spirit high. Its rich orange/blue flash streaking past on a boulder-strewn riverbank is a fleeting joy to behold. It heralds good news and gifts from unexpected quarters.

LARK: If ever there was a creature to exhibit the soaring, lofty heights of spiritual grace then the skylark must surely be top of the list. This little bird possesses, with its beautiful song and rapid ascending flight, the ability to aspire poets to great works. To dream of the lark is to feel nature's creative energy that resides deep within us all. It is the bird that links us to our spiritual essence and beyond. To the sad and disheartened it represents hope, to lovers it denotes fidelity and joy. Celebrate its vision!

LINNET: Another attractive little bird this is, However, not quite so popularised as the lark. The cock linnet's rosy breast is emblematic of summer days and childish enthusiasm. A beneficent countryside sign of happy events to come.

MAGPIE: "One for sorrow two for joy, three for a girl and four for a boy. Five for silver, six for gold, seven for a secret never to be told." The magpie is steeped in heaps of native folklore. Its striking black and white plumage is reminiscent of other creatures that connect with aspects of duality. The magpie's harsh raucous chatter is symbolic of malicious gossip; moreover, its vicious nest-robbing habits are intricately linked to aspects of human theft. It is not then a welcome vision to behold.

MOORHEN: Emblematic of quarrels and family disputes. Their aggressive behaviour towards intruders is symbolic of human territoriality and the will to repel invaders. To see them in A vision is a warning to defend one's position against enemies.

NIGHTJAR: This bird's nocturnal reclusive nature gives it a close link to the sinister. It denotes all that remains unknown or unseen. We must remember that sometimes we need to unleash ourselves to discover deeper, hidden levels of self that dwell within. The unknown should not always be feared for numerous inventions have been revealed through the brave experiments of many mystical pioneers. Unseen and unknown planes abound in occult teaching and philosophy. Their great potency being evidently clear when we look at the negative, monotheistic propaganda thrown at Pagan religions throughout the centuries by moralistic churchmen afraid of losing their flock. To fear these levels is to fear aspects of oneself. The nightjar would make an excellent totem for all brave psychonauts into the unknown. Those hardy souls who would liberate their self from the mundane to seek out the sacred mystical places residing within.

NUTHATCH: This small bird's habit of creeping up trees in search of insects is subconsciously like our incessant quest for knowledge. See it as a sign of progress and personal evolution through life.

OUZEL: Again, in a similar fashion to the last bird, the ouzel denotes the search for hidden knowledge. This bird however is a creature of watery places like rivers. Because of this link with water, it more properly connects with feminine, intuitive, nourishing, goddess aspects rather than the fertilising, masculine, god visage of self. For a man to see it in dreams is a sign of the anima, the feminine/sensitive essence residing within his being. For a woman it denotes the many rooms making up her feminine, instinctive self.

OWL: What the eagle is to the sun/sky god, the owl is to the lunar goddess. This mysterious bird of night traditionally stands for wisdom that is hidden and yet unknown. The Egyptians linked the owl to death and passivity. It is the power of mystery, magick and imagination. Naturally, it is easy to connect this bird to negativity, yet we should resist such a temptation. Out of life comes death, out of death we again see new life. The owl's association with moon goddesses like Hecate also connects with old crone/wise one aspects and ultimately divination. Do not fear the Owl but instead listen to its inner wisdom with a still, receptive mind!

OYSTERCATCHER: Bird of the wide-open spaces on lonely shorelines. Symbolic of life, liberation, and freedom from repressive influences. Its black and white coloration again like other birds/animals is linked to dualistic concepts in creation.

PARTRIDGE: This bird's alarming habit of waiting until one is virtually upon it before shooting off from cover gives rise to links with unexpected surprises. It denotes shock, moodiness and unexpected confrontations that crop up without warning. It can also be linked to aspects of chicken-like silliness because of its odd nature.

PEEWIT: Also known as the Lapwing or Green Plover. This bird is seen in huge flocks as winter closes in. It is significantly tied to feelings of continuity and social interaction. See it as a fine symbol of friendship and glad tidings to come.

PELICAN: Intimately conjoined with the sea and thus the subconscious mind. Their symbolism may be seen as being very much like that of the gannet.

PHEASANT: Strong connection here with luxury and opulence because of its beautifully coloured plumage. The pheasant, like the partridge, also shoots out from cover in alarming fashion so it may be tied to sudden shock etc. It is a powerful omen to be thrifty with financial/business dealings.
PIGEON: Symbolic of travel and the ability to communicate with others. Often heralds news that has been long in coming, possibly in the form of an important letter through the post.

QUAIL: Sign of minor successes and fair dealings with business associates. Symbolic of inheritance and gifts from afar. Altogether a very favourable omen.

RAVEN: This bird is a sign of death and ill omen. However, its countenance is not all negative. The Celts regarded it as a creature of divination. It was two Ravens that warned the hero god Lugh of the advancing forces of his enemies the Fomarian giants. The Norse god Odin had two Ravens, Hunin and Munin (thought and memory) that he sent out each morning to gather news of worldly events. Unfortunately, shallow Christian thinking demonised the poor old raven into a sign of the Devil. In Pagan philosophy life and death go hand in hand, as do aspects of divination and death. Samhain/Halloween is a prime example of this concept where life, death and prophecy conjoin. Death and divination are not evil they are essential rooms in the house of life. The raven exhibits this truth well. He comes to us as a vital warning not an evil enemy.

ROBIN: A sign of the approaching winter. Also symbolic of the life in death aspect inherent in the natural cycle. Its red breast is emblematic of hope in times of trouble, the bright spark of life that always eventually returns anew.

ROOK: Another symbol of death, obviously because of its coloration and crow-like nature. The rook also stands for family squabbles and disputes.

SHRIKE: The 'Butcher bird' as it is often called is emblematic of wanton cruelty and violence. Its grossly offensive habit of impaling victims on thorns and barbed wire leaves little to question its symbolic meaning. To see it in divination is not a favourable omen. I would also suggest that we could see in this bird associations with personal sacrifice to achieve one's aims. The old concept of self-sacrifice to assist others is certainly not of Christian origin. Many Pagan deities exhibited this trait long before the Jesus myth took hold of popular spiritual behaviour patterns. The shrike then links into this interesting mode of human thought process.

STARLING: The Starling is the perfect exemplification of ravishing greediness. These gluttons quickly devour every morsel on the bird table before smaller diners can even make an appearance. They stand for everything that is selfish and thoughtless toward others. If they have a saving grace in symbolism it must relate to the majestic beauty exhibited by their massive swirling flocks in winter. This spectacular sight is synchronised energy at its raucous best; energy that exemplifies the vital ebbing and flowing cycles of life. The old name for a starling was Shepster or Sheppy (Sheppie) because of the bird's habit of frequenting sheep pens to feed off the animals' resident ticks!

SWAN: In Celtic myth, Caer Ibormeith (the Gaelic Dream maiden) and her companions after each summer turn into Swans. Angus, the god of love, changed himself into a swan and flew away with Caer to his home, living happily ever after. Many other deities have been subject to mythological alteration into these beautiful birds. The swan then is an ancient native symbol of transformation, grace, and aspects of refined romance. White swans are emblematic of prosperity and true love, whilst black swans give us warning of forbidden romances that may ultimately lead to disaster.

TERN: The old colloquial name for the tern was 'Sea swallow' because of its swooping flight pattern and forked tail. This bird attacks its prey in a similar fashion to larger sea birds, diving from height to kill small food fish. It is a symbol of dynamic energy, enjoyment, and happy times to come.

THRUSH: This bird is symbolic of hope and good fortune. The beautiful, euphoric melody of a song thrush needs no introduction. Its pure voice is enough to gladden the most disconsolate of hearts. On the flip side of our symbolic coin there is however another side to the thrush. Its habit of cracking open snails on hard rocks stands as a sign of endurance and the ability to master life's smaller problems. The Mistle Thrush's old country name was 'Storm cock', gained through its strange custom of singing on the tops of high places such as church spires during a thunderstorm. The magickal feeling of spiritual renewal inherent in the thrush is quite plain to see, for all those seekers with open minds and hearts.

TURNSTONE: This ubiquitous little chap is often seen in massive flocks at the seaside, where it hunts quickly for marine creatures before the tide turns to invade its salty larder. Symbolically speaking, the turnstone represents anxiety mixed with optimism. It is a sign that one is trying too hard to reach goals that may be achieved in easier fashion. This bird may also frequent one's visions when we have lost something precious in life. Turning stones to discover our losses or alternatively to find new knowledge of self! Also significant of a change of lifestyle to come. Other fast little wading birds, such as sanderling, dunlin and knot, that inhabit the tideline also hold similar symbolic associations.

VULTURE: This ungainly scavenger is probably Africa's equivalent to our own carrion eating birds such as the crow. The vulture is the bird of death and destruction. To see it in vision is not usually a welcome sight although we must remember that death is an essential component in the universal cycle of life. Symbolically, vultures link with the Goddess in her darker, warlike, destroying, old hag aspect. On the masculine side of divinity, vultures were once given as offerings to the Roman god of war, Mars. Many pre-Christian peoples viewed this creature as a sign of reincarnation and vital, spiritual transformation because of its gross (but essential) corpse eating habits. Romulus and Remus founded Rome after seeing portents involving vultures. They believed that the presence of these birds would ensure the creation of a powerfully warlike nation. History testifies to their omen's great accuracy. We may shun the nastier side of life yet without it life would cease to exist. The vulture is a gift from the gods in vision, telling us to face hidden truths that we would prefer to ignore. The easiest way in life is not always the most beneficial path to follow. This bird can in spirit lead us into greater understanding of negative energies that must be challenged, in order to achieve balance and harmony.

WAGTAIL: A bird of beautiful places, especially the Yellow Wagtail and its relative the Grey Wagtail. Its habit of darting out from a rock to snatch a passing river fly is emblematic of our quest for universal knowledge. The river is symbolic of life drifting by, whilst we (as the wagtail) cast ourselves into the flow to grab what wisdom (the flies) we can along the way. The wagtail's frantic tail bobbing is also linked to ideas of impatience. This bird tells us to enjoy life by not allowing stress to become a problem. In other words, 'chill out and take it easy whenever possible!'

WOODPECKER: Picus, the Roman god of agriculture whilst out hunting one day in the forest came across the magickal goddess Circe, daughter of Sol. The goddess fell deeply in love with the handsome Picus, but alas the god could not return her feeling for he was already betrothed to Canens, daughter of the double - faced god of doorways, Janus. Circe's anger was consolidated at this refusal. So, after trying several fruitless methods to capture him she brushed the god with her wand, and he was instantly transformed into a Woodpecker. Legend has it that Picus was so outraged by his fate that he angrily flew into the trees and began pecking off the bark as still happens to this very day. The scientific, Latin name for this bird, Picidae, links us to the ancient woodland myth of transformation. Life is in fact not static at all, it is always altering and changing form. The woodpecker then is a symbol of essential life force metamorphosis of which we are all an inextricable part. In layman's language, the woodpecker is a sign that one's life may soon be about to alter in dramatic fashion. Expect changes.

WREN: The little Jenny Wren is surrounded by mystery, magick and legend. The Druidic priests of the Celts considered it to be a bird of divination. The origins for this belief in the wren's spiritual importance are exhibited in numerous Celtic stories. In ancient folklore the wren is the bird of the waning year, whilst the robin is given to be his opposite (waxing year) opponent. The traditional time for celebrating the wren's victory over the robin was at Winter Solstice (Yule). The wren once actually personified the waning year as people used to hunt it at that time in the calendar. This was a symbolic 'casting out' of the old year to make way for the new one to come. Vestiges of this custom are still found in Ireland today, where children gather on St Stephens Day (26th December) to make merry and visit neighbours' houses for reward. They are known as the 'Wren

Boys' because they carry with them the image of a Wren. Legend has it that a wren unfortunately landed upon a war drum belonging to the Danes, which alerted their guards just before they were surprised by the attacking Irish army. Since that fateful day, the local Irish people hunted the wren for its treachery. This is one reason given for the poor old wren's bad treatment under Irish hands. In Britain, the bird seems to have been given greater sanctity if we can believe the old West Country rhyme: "Whoso kills a Wran (Wren) shall never prosper boy or man." The wren and robin are plainly substituting for light and dark aspects of the Sun god, who is slain then reborn at summer and winter solstices. It would be difficult not to be moved by the delightful song of this tiny vocalist. Today the wren remains with us as a concise subconscious symbol of change and transformation of energy.

Before we depart from this short list of birds, the following comments may be advantageous. Magickal knowledge that we can acquire from birds must be experienced on an intimately personal level of spiritual understanding.

Generally speaking, 'third-hand' knowledge is usually quite unsatisfactory and, in the end, gets us nowhere at all. By interrelating with the beautiful sights and sounds of nature, we open our spirit and become purer, altogether greater beings. This fact applies to all spiritual matters and is the main reason why Pagans become their own priests/priestesses.

A thousand books cannot match one quiet summer's afternoon spent in the company of a woodland glade, full of singing birds. Their spirits can and do conjoin with our own (for the benefit of both parties) if we sincerely open our hearts and go along with the gentle cosmic flow.

BIRTH: Visions and dreams of birth may remain largely insignificant to women in a state of pregnancy. To have such visions at other periods of one's life is another matter altogether. The concept of birth is emblematic of new beginnings and happy events that may be totally unconnected with actual physical birth. Symbolically, birth marks a time of transformation, a time when energies take on new form. For a man in a hostile environment, it may depict a subconscious desire to return to the warm safety of the mother's womb. For a woman it may represent the desire (or fear) of pregnancy. Generally, if we must use that odd word, birth dreams precede happy events and changes for the better in one's fortunes.

BLACKBERRIES: Visions of berries or seeds are strongly connected to concepts about new ideas and growth. The matter of whether the idea is good or bad depends on the species in question. Although of course the dark coloration of edible blackberries links them to night, darkness and the negative principle. Traditionally, they were often seen as an unlucky sign, however they were also used in protective charms when gathered during the correct phase of the lunar cycle.

BLACKSMITH: Sign of persistence in overwhelming odds. If you see him in dreams then your ambitions will eventually be realised, albeit with much hard labour. The value of the smith was fully appreciated by our pre-Christian Celtic ancestors. Goibniu was the patron deity of this trade. The Tuatha De Danann (People of the goddess Danu) relied on him to craft their weapons to combat their sworn enemy, the Fomorians. Because of this ancient traditional link, we may also view the smith as a possible genetic omen of trouble to come that we must prepare for. Be on your guard, be ready and don't get caught out is the message from this sign.

BLOOD: The universal symbol of life and sacrifice. The sight of blood causes many people to collapse. The blood pressure drops, and unconsciousness comes to save the system from further distress. Blood can also cause panic and fear in numerous viewers, which again is a perfectly natural human survival reaction. Symbolically, blood is linked to new life and hope for a better future. The modern Christian sacrificial aspect of blood is nothing new. We can trace this element into the mists of time, as many earlier Pagan deities and their myths connect to this current of thought process. Blood links us to the concept of resurrection, reincarnation, and rebirth. The blood of Adonis/Attis was believed to be transformed into beautiful red poppies that filled the rich summer fields. His life fluid is again seen in the deep reddish hue of rivers falling after the seasonal floods. The menstrual cycle of the woman is also inextricably conjoined with the aspect of blood, as are the phases of the Moon. Modern horror writers were quick to realise the potential for blood's link to sexuality. Count Dracula's hypnotic gaze sexually stupefies his victim before he partakes of her vital life fluid. There is a very thin line between life and death; blood depicts this truth well. New life and cruel killing; sacrifice and resurrection of the soul. Yes, blood can be an omen of the worst or the best in human nature and we must listen to this essential message very well indeed.

BOAT: Anything that floats on the water is directly or indirectly connected with the mental faculty. To travel upon light seas denotes pleasant events forthcoming. Voyages in stormy waters are an omen of worries and troubles to come. To be flung into heavy turbulent seas from a boat is a warning to be aware of illness and mental problems.

BOLT: A sign of obstacles in one's progress through life. Can be a warning to liberate oneself from everyday drudgery and boredom especially if the bolt appears in a recurring dream.

BOMB: Symbol of pent-up rage (or fear) and suppressed emotions. Because of the explosive aspect, this vision is also strongly connected to sexual ejaculation and especially repressed sexuality. The dynamic principles of the bomb make it particularly significant in an adolescent/teenage (wet) dream state.

BONE: A sign of what rests behind the superficial egocentric self. To strip away the outer layers of the skin and expose the bones is to look within, toward many hidden (suppressed?) aspects of oneself. In essence, bones subconsciously denote the naked man/woman as nature intended them without the indoctrinated falsehoods of a materialistic society.

BOOK: Books are linked to wisdom, intelligence, harmony, and good fortune. They denote periods of calm that are necessary to combat everyday strains and stresses. Books in vision can be a sign from the gods to start a fresh, more beneficial lifestyle. Books are emblematic of spiritual prowess and the power to defeat evil. Also, divine secrets that are known to the select few, i.e., in olden times priests, being the only people who could read holy writ, would hold the spiritual monopoly over a naive populace. Wisdom always has a price; it is up to us to discover if this price is worth paying. 'Avoid the stress and enjoy life with less...' this must be the sensible watchword here.

BOOT: Because of its connection with the earth the boot/shoe sign is linked to travel. To see an old worn-out boot is symbolic of stagnation, lethargy, and depression in one's life. A new shiny boot denotes vitality and happy journeys to follow quite soon.

BOW: To draw a bow and to shoot an arrow is subconsciously linked to casting forth a thought or emotion into the void of life. The great god Apollo destroyed the serpent Python with his Bow and Arrow. The serpent had been sent by the goddess Juno to persecute Latona (Apollo's mother). The bow often features in mythology as an instrument of justice and vengeance. Most notable in popular consciousness as the (quite recent) Robin Hood legend for instance. It can also be seen today as a symbol of righting wrongs or putting old scores to rest. The bow is also symbolic of being love-struck as with Cupid's arrows of passion.

BOX: Symbolically, an analogous compartmentalisation of the mind. Whatever one discovers inside the box is what dwells within the deepest part of the human consciousness. Hopes and fears are all possible within the mysterious confines of the box. The obvious aspect of containment makes the box a feminine sign. Containment in this instance relating to the genital/sexual act and to burial. Respectively, both these encompassing aspects of the box link first to life i.e. - sexuality/containment and secondly to death as in coffin/burial - returning to the Goddess/Mother Earth.

BRANCH: Linked to all aspects concerning trees. Branches that appear wind - swept or broken are bad omens and may herald misfortune and accidents. To see branches bearing lush foliage or fruits is a particularly good sign of future prosperity.

BREAD: Good wholesome bread is a sign of family harmony and togetherness. The pragmatic Romans even had a goddess called Fornax who was given the task of presiding over the baking of bread. Visions of mouldy inedible bread are a harbinger of misfortune, illness, and poverty.

BREWING: To dream of brewing wine or beer is a good sign. Brewing and merriment often go hand in hand. The Roman god of wine was Bacchus and during his festivals the merrymakers would experience great fun and games. Such beverages have ancient sacrificial/religious associations. The contemporary wiccan rite of 'Cakes and Ale' and the Christian Transubstantiation (i.e., eucharistic elements believed to alter into blood of Christ) are the most recent examples of this mystical process. The sacrificial aspect of these fluids can be traced back into archaic mythology. For more on this subject see the above comments on blood.

BRICKS: Bricks are, of course, used to make walls thus they are a sign of subconscious barriers and taboos. They are also connected with building-shelters to house people so alternatively they may denote growth and increased finances. It is important to take careful note of surrounding signs when seeking to decipher such a seemingly contradictory symbol as this. To see bricks being smashed is symbolic of personal liberation from oppression and freedom of spirit.

BRIDE: A wedding featuring a beautiful happy bride is a grand omen. To see one in rags is a sign of misery and hardship. We can find links to the term Bride in the ancient Celtic goddess Brigit, who was also known as Brigid/Bride. This potent Gaelic deity was to be later canonised into Saint Bridget (450-523 ev) by cunning missionaries in Kildare, Ireland.

BRIDGE: Symbol of change from one state/place/level or emotion to another. Seeing a bridge in vision/dream, especially after a dispute, denotes the desire to repair the rift, hence the term, 'Building bridges!' Bridges are often places linked to danger that one must brave to get to a safer location, or level of understanding. The act of taking on that bridge can result in the death of the old, materialistic self as higher intelligence is gained. To cross a bridge with ease portends good fortune. Troublesome crossings foretell of disaster and ruination.

BROOM: An old Pagan sign of love and prosperity. Christianity deviously created the mediaeval, ugly witch/ hag on a broomstick stereotype image. This creation not only victimised innocent Pagan minorities but made sure that every lonely old woman was subject to vile defamation in society from that earliest witch burning period onwards. The origins for this cruel vilification probably arose from old fertility rites when unchurched villagers would sing and dance around the growing young spring crops. Part of the celebrations involved jumping to the height of a brush in hope that the local genius/spirit/deity of the corn would allow the harvest to grow to a similarly impressive zenith. The old Pagan, Hand Fasting (wedding) ceremony sometimes involved the happy couple leaping over a birch brush. Obviously, the puritanical Christians of the period saw this indigenous traditionalism as sexually immoral, which led to further defamation of native folklore, symbolism, and customs. To see visions of sweeping with a new broom denotes increasing benefit in finances or romance.

BROTHER: To a man this is a sign of competition/challenge. To a woman it is symbolic of companionship and helpfulness. Naturally, such a sign as this is wide open to personal interpretation, depending solely upon the family relationship of the subject in question.

BUBBLES: These can be a warning against being misused by others in whom we trust. Bubbles form a connection betwixt the realms of what is visible and the invisible. Therefore, they depict magick and the unknown. They link together the elements of water, air and finalise them by exploding into pure, unadulterated spirit. This symbol tells one to beware of fairy favours, that are like glory, little more than fleeting transpositions.

BUGS: Commonly seen as a sign of minor irritation or worry. Also, however a symbol of industrious activity and creative energy. This is especially so if the image is of an insect displaying social interconnections with others i.e., ants, termites, bees, wasps, etc. The two latter signs can obviously (because of their stinging nature) be warnings of ill health and discourse.

BUILDINGS: We subconsciously see dwelling places as extensions of our deeper self. To view a ramshackle house in vision is to see aspects of our innermost nature that we would rather keep hidden i.e., feelings of guilt, depression, fear, or anxiety. Buildings that appear clean and luxurious reflect feelings (or plans) of joy, peace, and contentment.

BURIAL: like the Death card in the Tarot's Major Arcana, this sign is not always as negative as it first appears. Burial is a return to the safety of Mother Earth, she who nourishes and protects us from harm. It is a sign of change, when one cycle ends another new one begins. This is sometimes symbolic of a deeper desire to leave the material world behind, to forge our being into greater heights of achievement.

BURNING: The creative divine spark that dwells within us all is often seen as fire. Fire destroys yet in its destruction it also creates anew. Materialistically, see it as a sign of increasing fortunes and energy. Spiritually, view it as the purifying light that connects us to the realm of the gods. The desire to become a better, more noble person. Horrific dreams of burning may result from a troubled or guilty conscience, especially if the dream or vision is persistently recurring. Alternatively, could be suggestive of death or injury in a previous, past life incarnation.

CAGE: The actual cage often resides within the viewer. To be trapped therein is a sign of frustration and anxiety. To break free is to liberate oneself from oppression and hardship, either created from communication with other people/circumstances or solely by one's own misplaced efforts. The first thing to do if cages appear in vision is to relax and closely scrutinise one's situation for faults. The gods can only warn, we must provide the ears to listen and the eyes to see.

CAKE: An exceptionally good sign of happy events to come. The cake is the effort of labour and ingredients necessary to create harmony; as such it foretells beneficent relationships and fair balance in life. A great time for new projects to begin.

CALL: To hear one's name distantly shouted (even though the caller is not there) in the small hours, often suddenly jerks us into fully waking consciousness. A similar event arises when we have a nightmare about falling downstairs. We wake up in a cold sweat, thankful that we are not actually harmed in any fashion. This type of dream is typical of the mind changing its focus from the mundane, waking, level to the dreamworld of vision and fantasy. The everyday mindset is resisting its journey into the netherworld, just like a reluctant dental patient fighting off the effects of the operative's anaesthetic gas. The mind can be extremely conservative, not wishing to change from one level of focus to another. The call then, is a panic button, which arises from a highly active mental level, unwilling to change into a lower gear. If the caller is seen and known, then it may be a warning to beware of danger approaching soon. If it comes from a known deceased person, then regard it as possible direction from the spirit world and examine your situation constructively, with care.

CAMERA: On the materialistic level this is a token warning that someone in whom you trust is not as sincere as they may have first appeared. This is especially so if it is they who point the camera at you. You are being scrutinised in a cold, uncaring manner and your subconscious is telling you this fact very clearly indeed. On deeper astral levels the camera is a symbol of one's consciousness. We use the lenses as we use our conscious focus, zooming from one subject (awareness) to another. The camera then is a vehicle that allows us in vision/dreams to shift from one place to another in the fastest possible time.

CANAL: Water of any kind links with the subconscious mind set and canals are no exception. Peaceful canals surrounded in natural beauty are representative of inner peace, or at least the desire for such a blessing. Derelict canals that are grey and polluted herald poverty and illness. The latter is a sure warning to change direction in life or face the uncomfortable consequences soon to be experienced.

CANDLE: The light in the darkness and thus illumination of spirit. The flickering flame of a candle is virtually timeless. It depicts the divine spark in us all, the power of creation in which we all inherently share. An unlit candle stands for disappointment and delay. The flame that is absent represents helplessness and the inability to venture forth into desired places, on many levels.

CANE: Very much a cultural sign this one. To some the cane is a symbol of authority and discipline, especially those persons who see (or saw) fit to use it to inflict pain on their minions. Obviously to the receiver it is symbolic of brutality, harsh authority and abuse of power. Also stands for religious intolerance against minorities seen as a threat to holy writ. Leaving the physical side, it is emblematic of the element of wood. Wood increases and thus the cane also stands for new ideas and future success.

Cards

CARDS: Playing cards (esp. face cards) represent the quintessential aspects of the human condition. The following loosely based inventory may prove helpful to readers although the subject itself is of course wide open to personal interpretation. Incidentally, it is worth remembering that the modern pack of playing cards links closely with elemental qualities and the antediluvian mystery, which we know today as the Tarot.

KING OF HEARTS: Authority, albeit connected with the emotional state of mind. Romantic involvements are predominant in the field of vision displayed by this sign. In the negative connotation it serves as a warning of marriage rifts and love squabbles.

KING OF DIAMONDS: Again authority, but this time belonging to the realms of earthly matters such as current relationships, business ventures and financial position. Worldly events.

KING OF SPADES: Represents that which is manifest in physical form or is soon to become so. A stern/no nonsense figure who expects discipline and obedience from those belonging to his entourage. Also, a warning that health matters should be watched with care. A threatening man.

KING OF CLUBS: Creative situations are evident with this symbol. Expect advice (either good or bad) relating to important matters of inspiration or artistic interpretation when the King of Clubs appears before you.

QUEEN OF HEARTS: Like the King of this suit, she is emblematic of matters close to the heart. She stands for affection/grace/true love and exciting new romance.

QUEEN OF DIAMONDS: This lady brings us good news from the Goddess herself. She represents all that is fruitful in manifest earthly form. This queen gives evidence of wealth residing in (or coming to) the social/cultural infrastructure of one's life.

QUEEN OF SPADES: A lady of sharp contrast to the previous queens. She is the strict school mistress/the sad widow/the vitriolic landlady and the trenchant mother. This queen is a personification of the dark side of the feminine aspect, which is of course just as essential as the lighter half. She is the Cold Hag of winter, the purifying East wind and drives away all those who stand in her icy path.

QUEEN OF CLUBS: Here is a vision of great new beginnings. She forms a bridge between the known and unknown planes. The Queen of Clubs is the illumination needed to surmount obstacles that at first seem too difficult to conquer.

JACK OF HEARTS: A vital person filled with love for life and others. He is the good friend, the kind brother and the loyal lover. To see him in vision is most beneficent and one should expect an important blessing to arrive soon after.

JACK OF DIAMONDS: A materialistic type of sign this, although not in any derogatory way. He is very much a messenger from the gods, bringing news from higher levels into the conscious realm so that we may understand greater awareness.

JACK OF SPADES: This card represents the pioneer and the adventurer. Action all the way and new exciting opportunities can be expected when this image appears to you. There is however sometimes a curt warning in this card, relating to health matters should not be overlooked.

JACK OF CLUBS: A fiery sign that links with everything that is energetic and full of exuberance. A herald that tells us to "Go for it." Any important endeavour that has been delayed should now be launched with full steam ahead! Don't put off any new business/social or romantic enterprises any longer. Now is the time to act and win the day!

Negative - Positive?

When is the card's symbolism to be viewed positively or indeed negatively, you may rightly ask? I'm afraid the answer to this quite logical question can only come from you dear reader. It can also only come from that deep, dark inner pool, where logic wanes and the seemingly illogical, magickal, mindset takes over.

One of the saddest features of modern life is the way in which everyone expects somebody else, i.e., the priest/holy man to answer their questions for them. Have none of this lazy spiritual slumber, take the bull by the horns

51

and seek your own truths. Become your own priest/ess. Find your own answers to life's mysteries.

Never ever leave your precious spiritual birthright in the hands of another human being for they may be lower on the evolutionary path of spirit than you first realised. Your truth is a most superb gift from the gods, do not ever insult them by neglecting it, or giving it away!

In a rather simplistic manner, modern playing cards link with the Tarot in the following way:

Hearts = Cups
Diamonds = Pentacles/Coins
Spades = Swords
Clubs = Wands/Staves

HEARTS: In their symbolic formation hearts are of course always represented with a concave or cup-shaped dorsal surface. The idea of cupping/holding connects with the maternal image and thus also links with aspects of love (The Loving Cup of old.) Like emotions, waters flow, so it is simple to see just why hearts/cups conjoin here and result in romantic sign language. With hearts we are dealing with more astral levels of reality. We are talking here of emotions and feelings that have not yet developed into solid physical matter.

DIAMONDS: Found in the bosom of Mother Earth, diamonds are hard shiny and beautiful. Their hardness links with the logical, conscious, solid mindset that operates within the bounds of the materialistic earth plane. Coins connect with everyday things that remind us of existing worldliness. Pentacles fit into this equation too. They are usually fashioned from metals and represent the earth element on the witch's altar. Diamonds and pentacles/coins connect us to the sublunary realm, where higher planes of existence have become manifest into the solid matter of physical reality. They are manifestation personified.

SPADES: A spade moves earth and as such in symbolic terms they modify an important aspect of reality. Spades/swords cut through air, an element that they usually represent. Thus, they cut through ideas and indecision, bringing light where before only darkness reigned supreme. It must be mentioned here however that some adherents feel safer with swords under the banner of fire element. The air-cutting sword and the earth-delving spade bring the material world into sharp focus. Reality of the unknown becomes knowable when this sharp sign comes into view. It is the personification not of the manifest but what is about to become so quite soon.

CLUBS: Clubs are fashioned out of wood, a natural substance that burns so well, inadvertently feeding and nourishing the earth from whence it first originated. We see here why confusion sometimes occurs as to which element clubs, or should we say wands, are really connected to. The burning aspect magnetises to the idea of brightly illuminated thought and intelligence. The club/wand is the partner of hearts. This is because again we are talking with this sign in an astral sense, rather than the material planes. Both hearts and clubs have intercourse with the emotional level, yet clubs pull more to the spirit of pristine adventure than to the passion felt in the hearts/cups suit.

I suggest the following links between the four suits, levels of manifestation and relevant god force therein:

Hearts/Cups: love/emotion/the maternal. Venus.

Diamonds/Pentacles: the earth/the physical. Mars.

Spades/Swords: etheric link betwixt manifest and astral. Jupiter.

Clubs/Wands: intellect/spirit/originality Mercury.

As I have said before, symbolic interpretation is a personal matter. Follow the intuition given to you by the gods with the cards as in everything else in life, and you will not go far from the path of true enlightenment.

Your truth is your essential link to the gods. You and you alone must discover it for yourself.

CASTLE: The fortress that contains treasure is symbolic of hidden mysteries. The castle depicts that which may sometimes be feared yet, which also holds a curiously mystical attraction. It is the gateway to other worlds/lands that lie beyond the known levels of consciousness in faraway dimensions of time, reality and space.

CATERPILLAR: Very symbolic of childhood. Small things that fascinate the immature mind sometimes get forgotten, but never quite completely. Caterpillars hold the secret of transformation from one state of being to another. They tell us to prepare ourselves for big changes to come.

CATHEDRAL: To the monotheistic-minded individual these vast structures stand for high ideals and illusions of spiritual grandeur. To those persons of a pantheistic worldview cathedrals are temples of suppression against native culture and repression of indigenous races. The positive/negative aspect of course being dependent upon one's socio-religious genealogy and current position in society. What is utterly sacred to one individual is deeply profane to another and vice versa. The positive side of this image is majesty, enlightenment and illumination, the negative being infiltration, loss, subversion, and religious genocide.

CAVE: The home of the unknown, the place where we face our inner fears and conflicts. Dark foreboding caves are (like castles) gateways to other interior/exterior dimensions. The underworld that we may enter to face a challenge, in order to seek greater enlightenment.

CEMETERIES: On the physical level we perceive cemeteries as places of sadness, loss, and remembrance. Death however in all his gloomy countenance is to the deeper mindset not quite that simple. Death is not an end; it is an adventure. We are an important composite aspect of the spiritual whole of creation and creative energy. This energy (the divine spark) that propels us is not destroyed at the time of death. Although we leave behind our physical frame, we liberate that force which we call in our ignorance the spirit. Just as a tadpole sheds its old self to transform into the frog, we too must return to the cosmic source to be improved and reborn again into the next vital incarnation. Within the inexperienced mind this knowledge seems often to be lacking, especially in his/her conscious worldview. However, the subconscious mind of even the most materialistic type of person usually realises more than we give it credit for. The deeper mind knows and tells us that visions of death/cemeteries are omens of change, which are not necessarily always conjoined with actual physical death. They can be signs that one's life is about to change drastically. They frequently herald the end of one phase and commencement of another, which may be beneficial.

CHAINS: All the life problems that we often perceive as actual mental burdens can manifest on the astral level as chains of one sort or another. We usually allow this negative situation to come into existence by our own wrong thinking. At times we are all guilty of this no matter how spiritually mature we may be. Chains then in vision are symbols of oppression that is often self-inflicted. Although of course outside influences may impinge upon us too, bringing subjugation and gross pessimism to an otherwise optimistic countenance. If you see chains in dreams, then it is time to critically examine with care your own perception of the world, and other people, about you. Recall the chains of Jacob Marley's ghost in the novel 'A Christmas Carol' by Charles Dickens, he fashioned the shackles himself!

CHALICE: The cup of emotion and spiritual enlightenment. Chalices and goblets abound throughout myth and legend, one of the most recent being the Holy Grail of Arthurian fame. The semi-mythical King Arthur story became a Norman romancer's Christianisation of much older native Pagan tales of the old gods. The Grail story of course belongs to this ancient indigenous pedigree. We have already spoken of the link betwixt cups/hearts and love. Chalices too make their mark within this equation. When we see this sign in vision, we may be perceiving a message from the gods telling us that life is soon to take on a greater degree of spirituality. The chalice is, for a younger person, an important herald of love and desire for fulfilment. The more maturely- minded individual may see it as a symbol of the higher self that seeks to link us to divinity. This is the greater spiritual awareness or intelligence that dwells deep within us all, what the ancient Romans knew intimately as the 'Genius'.

CHARIOT: Symbolic of war gods like Mars and Ares. This is a dynamic sign that life is about to take on greater momentum possibly for the better. The chariot is very much a symbol of conquest/victory over negativity and bravery in the face of seemingly overwhelming adversity. Also travel and dramatic change!

CHESS: The mark of a truly dualistic mind. The fight betwixt light and dark and good against evil. This vision depicts a battle in one's life that the subconscious has condensed into a smaller more easily understood form. The board is life while the pieces stand for certain actions that take place therein. Losing or winning at chess of course heralds positive or negative events to come into force soon.

CHIMNEY: Long tapering chimneys may be phallic symbols, suggesting that the dream/vision may be connected to sexuality. On deeper planes they can also be firm signs of religiosity; solid materialistic structures reaching upward to penetrate the heavens thus man having connection with the gods. A good sign in general.

CIRCLE: A symbol of eternity, infinity and the sacred Goddess and God. Our earliest folk memories originate from distant times when mankind held that great life giver, the Sun, in highest esteem. The Moon too, that firm sign of the Lunar Goddess in all her full glory has a long history in our psychic development as a species on this planet. Incidentally, Kitanitowit the supreme creator god of the Algonkin (Algonquin) Indians is often represented as a full circle because he represents the whole world and everything in it. The solar, lunar, and planetary aspects remind us of the complete circle. The circle is one of the strongest life signs we possess and to see it in vision/meditation is a very firm herald of increased vitality, dynamism, and optimism. The circle, like life, really has no beginning or end. It marks a constant flow of force and energy that can be changed but never actually destroyed.

CITY: To see a busy city where everything is grimy and chaotic is a sign of mental torpor, indecision, and anxiety. To view a city as shiny, new, and flourishing bodes well for future business and social enterprises that one may be planning.

CLOCK: Our earliest markers of time were of course the Sun and the Moon. Four weeks being one month or 'moonth, as it should be more correctly called. The sign of the clock is a sign of waiting. It is only natural for man to want power over time yet in many materialistic ways this remains an insurmountable obstacle. Time is like physical death because it is something that we cannot defeat. The clock then is symbolic of our hopes and fears over life and death. The ancient Roman god Janus was usually portrayed with two heads facing opposite directions. One looked to the future whilst the other marked the past. Janus, as a keeper of sacred time, holds the key to many questions including those connected to time.

CLOUDS: Dark foreboding clouds are signs of trouble and hardship, whilst blue sky and high white cloud is a good herald of imminent prosperity after stern challenges. Clouds represent thoughts drifting across the landscape of our mind.

COAT: Protection and all aspects relating to it. The coat is a layer that shields us from the elements. In dreamtime it represents a defence against whatever is threatening the dreamer. To lose a coat is to fear loss of a part of one's personality or character. If a friend or relative loses their coat this denotes trouble or illness for that person. Torn coats mean that hardship, disgrace, despair, or strife may be close at hand. Time to fortify one's defence.

COIN: In mundane terms symbolic of material wealth. However, coins hold more mystery on deeper levels than we may at first realise. Gold coins stand for the solar orb and the logical/conscious physical world, whilst silver ones depict the feminine/intuitive level connected with magick and the moon. Brass or copper-coloured coins connect with the earth and lower planes of existence. Shiny coins symbolise success, but dirty or dull ones foreshadow failure, anxiety, or sickness.

COMET: A glorious sign of revelation and inspiration. The comet is divine spiritual power manifesting on the physical plane. There is however a more sinister side to this vision. Comets in history have often been seen as harbingers of doom and disaster. In April 1066, the appearance of Halley's Comet in the night's sky, filled the common folk with dread and prophecies of evil were given by the wise. England's sorry fate at the hands of the victorious Normans later that year, along with the radical suppression of Saxon lifestyle is of course now well known. It certainly makes you think!

COMPASS: To see a spinning needle in a compass is representative of anxiety and indecision. A steady compass means that the right answer to pressing questions will soon be found. Seeking new directions in life may very well start with the sign of the compass!

COPPER: This metal whilst beautiful is of course somewhat inferior to gold. It is the tarnished face of the Sun and as such belongs to the lower levels of existence. In occult terms copper has associations with the great Goddess Venus and all things connected to love/lust/beauty. Copper then is a sign of the sexual nature of things, and this is especially true in a young person's dream/vision.

CORK: A strong and popular sign of celebration and family joys. Expect news of weddings or births to come into your realm quite soon. Corks floating on top of water mark one's struggle in life to challenge adversity.

CORN: To be involved in the harvest denotes friendship and happy events to come. Running corn through one's fingers is a sign of financial success and inheritance. Running in golden fields of corn is symbolic of total unadulterated liberation from the heavy shackles of mundane, worldly problems.

CORPSE: Symbolic of unhappy events to come and general pessimism. This is a warning to be on your guard against wrongdoers and criminals. It is also a warning to watch out for minor health problems that may escalate into major troubles. Like the sign of death in the Tarot it can sometimes herald important changes in life, which may eventually (after a struggle) be for the better.

CROSS: A sacrificial sign for obvious reasons. Also representative of punishment, death, and humiliation. A balanced, four-armed cross denotes equilibrium whilst one with unequal arms marks a period of discord and unease.

Incidentally, this old truth is well represented in the equal and unequal crosses, gyfu & nyd, of the runic Futhork (Futhark). Also, a directional sign, originally marking the four points of the compass. To a traveller it may be symbolic of decisions that must be made – which direction to take!

DAGGER: Be wise in your choice of friends for one may not be as trustworthy as you first believed; this is the hidden message conveyed here. Daggers, swords and knives link with the element of air, although some prefer to join them to the realm of fire. The cutting or rather penetrating aspect of these weapons gives them a connection with masculinity. This is then very much a phallic emblem and represents the fertilising nature of man. Daggers/knives also give rise to ideas of intrusion, shock and unwanted favours or attentions from others.

DANCE: Sign of freedom from oppression and liberation of the true self. Also, a token of celebrations and increasing sexuality, especially in younger persons. A sign in life!

DARKNESS: To see naught but the dark can warn of ill times ahead, yet we need to remember that without the dark there can be no light. Without chaos there can never be absolute harmony. Everything has its opposite, and we must remain philosophical in this sure knowledge. Like they say, "every cloud has its silver lining!" Although at a bad time this may be of little consolation.

DEATH: To dream of a long dead person may foreshadow an important event. This spirit has perhaps come to offer us help. It is our free choice whether we wish to accept it. The mind still retains much of its everyday logic in dreams. However, to understand this logic we must remember that symbolism is the name of the game in dreamtime. Thus, any questions we may have answered by a spirit will probably be conveyed in the forms of signs. To dream that one is dead marks a strong desire to escape mundane reality and all problems therein. Death may come not as an end but a whole new beginning. It stands for changing energies on all levels of existence.

DESERT: Hardships and strife may be near when we see this vision. The desert destroys moisture leaving only arid wasteland. The wasteland in question may possibly be one's deep self that is longing for some type of assistance and support from life's troubles. A change of career or relationships might be the answer here. Excessive solar power kills on the desert so overindulgence as a causative factor might be suggested by the subconscious in this vision. Avoidance of overdoing things is indicated.

DIAMOND: This is often a particularly good sign that events are soon to improve quite dramatically on the physical plane. For more insight on this interesting symbol please see the list on cards in this book.

DIVE: To dive into clear blue water portends a happy situation ahead, especially on the mental level. To enter dark foreboding water augurs a decline in one's welfare. The most important thing to remember is that water usually represents an aspect of the deeper mind. The everyday consciousness (the diver) plunges into the water (subconscious levels) so the actual state and clarity of the water relates to the mental harmony/balance of the dreamer.

DOOR: A powerful sign of journeys to other places. These places may however be not of the physical world but the spiritual. To step through a doorway into a darkened room is symbolic of entering the deeper mind. What we find in the room gives us a clue to whatever problems the subconscious is directing our attention to. We ignore these signs at our peril, particularly if the vision/dream is recurring. A door that cannot be opened is symbolic of hidden problems and anxiety.

DRUM: An important event in one's life is soon to take place. The question standing is whether the dreamer can face what is to come or not!

DWARF: To see other persons surrounding you in the form of dwarves, marks delusions of grandeur and feelings of superiority. If the vision shows you as a dwarf amongst giants, then the reverse is the case.

EARS: Some disrespectful individual is spreading malicious gossip behind your back. Ears are flapping at your expense; thus, you need to find out who the culprit is quickly. Beware of jealous spies amongst your associates.

EARTHQUAKE: Warning of momentous events soon to occur in one's life. May also of course relate to worldwide strife and aggression. Without wishing to sound too pessimistic, this sign is not one to be taken lightly. Health should be given high priority following this dangerous vision.

EGG: Portends new beginnings, money and fresh opportunities arising soon. Also denotes birth for obvious reasons. To fry eggs is to play with (hatch) vital new ideas. To see broken/rotten eggs is to lose temporary control of a tricky situation. May also denote need for security.

ENGINE: The engine is analogous with the vital life essence within man. Fast engines denote busy lifestyles and hectic events ahead. Sluggish engines herald boredom/ill-health and lost opportunities. Slow engines sometimes link with composure and contentment.

EYE: Like the ears this is a warning to beware of deceitful actions from others. You are being watched by someone who certainly does not have your best interests at heart. In a lighter vein, eyes can suggest that an admirer is hoping to catch your attention even though you have not consciously realised this fact just yet. One way or another – you are being scrutinised!

FAIRY: A symbol of our rich Pagan culture and heritage. In a layman's terminology generally a beneficent sign. Also marks the deep desire to return to a simpler, more natural world - far away from the hustle and bustle of modern society.

FALLING: Often, when we first enter the sleep process the active conscious mind resists the pull of slower deeper realms by jerking us out of our slumber with situations involving falling (i.e., off cliffs/buildings, stairs, etc.) Also portends a downward spiral in one's business and social dealings.

FATNESS: Traditionally often given as a sign of wealth, abundance, and even fertility. In today's easier (survival wise) more affluent society, fatness can be a psychological substitute emblem for sloth, greed, and apathy. Also symbolic of loss of control and the desire to become more attractive.

FENCE: A barrier that stands in your way to higher goals. To break down a fence in dreamtime and walk through it is to overcome life obstacles. To trip over/into one denotes accidents and mishaps ahead. Fences are walls standing in your way, break them down and move on!

FIELD: The actual state of the field and what is growing in it (if anything) gives the clue to the dream or vision. Lush green pastures denote contentment and easier times to come, whilst black fields of war and destruction forewarn us of strife and misery. The field is like the sea often analogous with the subconscious mind and everything dwelling within.

FIRE: This element must be esteemed very well indeed, for danger is never far from its grasp. Fire can nevertheless be a beneficent vision representing great passion, energy, and new growth. Fire is essential to our existence like all the other elements, because without its vigorous force to stir our emotions we would be much lesser creatures of this earth. We should always pay it deep respect and never take it for granted, on any level of existence. Fire is also a sign of inspiration.

FISHHOOK: A chance opportunity is coming your way, which you would be foolish to ignore. Do not let it slip away or you will have to live with the consequences. The gods can be critical and sometimes refuse us a second bite of the cherry.

FLOWER: A multi-complex subject which is beyond the scope of any small list. Flowers are generally emblematic of progress and affluence. However, colour plays an important role in identifying their symbolic meaning. Red flowers signify unbridled passion and sexual quests. Black or wilted ones are for negativity, loss, and sorrow. Pink ones denote romance, love, and attraction. Blue flowers denote intellect and logical mindset. White blossoms stand for purity, virginity, the new spring and sometimes sadness too. Yellow ones mark remembrance, calmness, and solitude. Purple flowers represent power, authority, and control.

FLYING: Liberation, freedom from oppression, hope for better times and joy. Flight brings forth to mind all these feelings and such a vision may be evidence of the need to open one's true self to a greater, more spiritual lifestyle. Flight can also be experienced in astral travel. As a child I had many beautiful visions/dreams of flying high over local buildings/trees etc. I passionately believe now that the wonderful aerial sights that I saw were actual, yet involuntary, journeys of my astral body that had left the physical realm behind.

FORTRESS: A large impenetrable fort that cannot be breached is symbolic of increasing problems and major worries in security. To be in a fortress overlooking other mortals shows delusions of grandeur and frequently gives evidence of an inferiority complex in the making. The latter may seem a strange, even contrary suggestion at first mention. Surely, you may rightly ask, standing over others in dominance is a sign of victory and power? That may be so at face value however those who feel a strong need to dominate their fellows are but spiritual children with all the same hidden insecurities within. The wise person does not compete!

FROST: Beautiful, alluring, and full of wonderment yet at the same time holding the threat of danger and mishap. This aspect of nature is deified by every mother/grandmother for her kin. "Wrap up warm so that Jack Frost can't get at you." Familiar words to many a small child facing the cold winter's journey to school. I remember seeing the serious look descend upon my young niece's face when told this by her granny. A mixture of excitement tempered with thoughtful apprehension set in, which epitomised this sign's message so very accurately indeed. The runic symbol for ice is called 'Isa' or 'Is,' (the latter being Anglo Saxon) and it portrays the energy of frost very successfully. Admire its charm yet beware the dangers lurking within. One slip and all that glistening beauty may suddenly seem less than perfect. In a nutshell, look to your health and take precautions. I sneezed twice as I wrote this very line; it's a frosty day too. Isn't life strange? Ah well, out with the lemons and hot water!

FUR: Here's another sign like fatness that is going through a cultural revolution. Traditionally symbolic of affluence and gross materialistic luxury, the mink coat once being the status mark of every hope-filled aspiring film-star. Now, thanks to the proliferation of anti-fur animal rights organisations in society, fur has become emblematic with greed, cruelty, and selfishness. Naturally, our values as a civilised structure change. Once it was essential for man to steal fur from animal corpses to survive the cold months.

However, today it is not necessary. There are now many better man-made materials readily available. Fur then is on one hand a symbol of our Neolithic past which evolved into quite recent times as a mark of power and wealth. On the other hand, it is now mainly a token sign of avarice and one-upmanship. Possibly a warning from the gods to stop being self-centred and consider others. If you don't take heed, you may regret it!

GALE: Sign of a troubled mind. To be blown away is to lose control of the situation. Time for a major rethink regarding business, financial and social affairs. New events ahead which may be highly significant to you.

GARDEN: A place of great harmony and contentment. To see a tidy one in dreams is a good omen for future happiness and fulfilment. Unkept gardens may portend sadness, or the desire to escape social problems.

GHOST: To see an apparition in vision is often a warning to tread carefully for danger is at hand. This is especially so if the spectre is known to you as a lost relative or friend.

GLOVES: This image denotes the need for protection and care. It also warns us not to be cajoled into foolish situations by extroverted timewasters and gossips. Can also denote a serious challenge to your self-esteem. The glove also covers the hand thus it may represent hidden intentions being mounted against you.

GRAPES: A good sign of wealth and plenty. Also, a signal that a difficult project is soon about to come to fruition.

GRASS: Like sea/land/sky etc., any large grassy expanse in dreams frequently parallels the subconscious mindset. Green healthy-looking grass is comparable with clear logical thinking. Alternatively, poor darkened matted grasses relate to turmoil, stress, and anxieties.

GUITAR: Soft melodious playing arises from seductive and romantic desires, whereas aggressive loud music marks out the more troubled, immature, mind and the need for liberation. Time to give freedom to pent up wishes and unshackle yourself from the stifling situation which surrounds you!

GUN: Primarily an unstable yet dominant priapic symbol in the male. In the female they denote a deep desire for social attention, love, or sexual relationships. Guns are equivalent to expensive sports cars, because they symbolically display the immature need to project (or protect) a weakened ego to be noticed. They are a status symbol for the owner/dreamer. Consider the proud peacock showing off his bright plumage and you will get the same inherent message. Possibly psychologically suggestive of inordinate sexual stimulation, or even premature ejaculation. Also, a token emblem of sudden disastrous occurrences, which may test one's abilities to the full. Beware of cunning enemies posing as good friends, for skulduggery is close at hand!

HAMMER: Much depends on the light in which the hammer is viewed. To break rocks with one means that you will win through problems after a hard struggle. To see one in the sky is a good herald of excellent opportunities coming soon. The hammer that sparks is a sign of creative/divine inspiration; your life will take on a new meaning. A blessed mark of the Thunder god in all his multifarious guises. Also intricately connected with the god of fire, Vulcan. An open-minded individual will quickly discover further links here between the sacred hammer, passion, and the emotions within.

HAND: A hand with fingers pointing at one, tells us to think well about our proposed course of action. The gods in their wisdom are warning us to analyse a situation, which may seem satisfactory but is quite dangerous in some way. A raised open palm tells us to stop and think because plans may go astray. Hands are, like faces, physical expressions of emotional force. They act as great guides and sometimes guardians too. In the realm of dreams and vision, don't ever ignore them.

HARP: Love and romance are never far away from this sign. There is however a certain amount of pent-up stress/emotion inherent in the harp's arduous structural composition. The love aspect is evident in the Swan-like form of the harp. The Swan is very intricately linked with the Celtic god of love and beauty, Angus. His father the Dagda possessed a wooden harp, which played all by itself and brought the seasons into order. Angus too had a harp yet unlike his father's instrument it was made of gleaming gold. When Angus played it was impossible to resist the charm of his sweet melodies. The harp then is an ancient part of our native cultural romance. Without doubt it forms an excellent harbinger of love and longing passions aroused.

HELMET: A symbol that underscores associations with the higher intellect or even spirituality. The helmet covers that part of oneself which is prized by many as the centre of being. An open helmet signifies trustworthiness, whilst a closed visor gives rise to sinister intentions against the viewer by some other unknown party. Time to be careful!

HERBS: Herbs are too wide a ranging subject to lump together under one generalisation. However, for the sake of simplicity, I shall state that they link subconsciously with the psyche. Any substance that possesses the ability to heal or kill impresses the human mind much more than we realise at face value. Herbs connect, because of this aspect of wonder, to myth, legend, and most of all to magick. No Pagan rite would be complete without its correct portion of herbs, either for use in incense of otherwise. Each plant is anciently connected to a different godform or planetary virtue. For example, dill, fern, and marjoram lie beneath the dominion of Mercury, whilst Venus claims the possession of golden rod, elder and the sorrels.

HILL: Green pleasant hillsides in summer tells us that any problems faced in life will soon be conquered. The inability to overcome difficult hills means that there is a strong chance of unwelcome attentions from other individuals soon.

HOOD: Secrets of the mind and beyond abound when the hood comes into vision. Like the helmet, this is a head covering yet the hood occludes all facial features. It hides the true emotions thus prevents the viewer from knowing what lies beneath. The hood can be a positive image i.e., the hooded (heroic) figure of Robin Hood. Alternatively, it may be negative having associations with dread, fear, and the realms of death. For instance, the hooded terror of the Inquisition's priestly torturers or even the black, apocalyptic image of the hooded, Grim Reaper. The hood then encourages us to discover something that's unknown, something that we must eventually face that is presently hidden from our common worldly perception.

HORNS: Horns are an ancient sign of fecundity/sensuality. To see them in dreams is an omen of sexual prowess in a man and fruitfulness in a woman. The early church took all the ancient Pagan horned gods of nature i.e., Pan/Cernunnos/Faunus etc., which represented the essential fertilising life force and transformed them into satanic forces. The council of Toledo defined the Devil to have cloven hooves and a horned head (Pan?) in 447 AD. Thus, essentially natural personifications of fertility were twisted into evil by the sex-hating church fathers sitting in their lofty positions of absolutist power. Psychologists/healers and sex counsellors are still dealing with the inherent consequences of this old theocratically inspired crime against nature. The sad monotheistic doctrine against natural, life-creating passion/fertility has fostered more sexual guilt complexes on the world's naive populace than grains of sand on a beach.

Naturally, (or should we say unnaturally?) those affected by this type of subconscious, religious mind manipulation will always gravitate, like moths to a lantern, towards the very source that creates their ongoing problems. Consequently, the problem continues unabated throughout history. The intolerant clergy that foster this sexual misinformation, happily comfort desperate adherents of the faith by simply offering yet more of the same, tired old anti-life, anti-sex theocratical nonsense. This results in complexes and insecurities being hidden deeper and deeper in a sea of dogmatic platitude. Woe betides any liberated freethinker who dares to even question this twisted situation for they will be immediately cold shouldered and treated as an evil heretic or radical. Thus, the old guilty (sex is dirty) thought form, which has now actually developed its own quasi-independent existence, protects itself from invasion. Such is the insidious nature of mind-control of the converted masses. Horns and their symbolism are of course not inherently evil. They are a vital relic of a prehistoric time when early man thought his own thoughts instead of having them injected into his brain by a power-seeking priesthood, intent on having its own way. Ironically, the lamb has become the force for destruction of our free will, not those theocratically abused horned creatures holding the wondrous power of life, love and liberation depicted so well in the image of the Horned One. Sadly, Christian doctrine generated the unnatural Satanic concept. Society is still trying to pull itself out of the spiritual morass caused by this dangerous thought form. This manmade, illusion has disrupted the psychic balance of life and the sooner it is abandoned by us the better it will be for our species as a whole!

HORSESHOE: Old sign of wonder and magick. Iron that fashions the horseshoe has magickal associations. It was thought to ward off mischievous fairies/elves. The shape of the shoe is crescent-like, as in the moon, so naturally it acquired a certain empathy with lunar deities such as Diana, Hecate, and Luna. Incidentally, Epona is the Romano/Celtic horse goddess, so we should also remember this powerful deity's association traditionally encapsulated within this old symbol. The horseshoe remains in popular human consciousness as the perfect embodiment of good luck and psychic protection.

INK: To spill ink is a warning against libel, either by the viewer or directed against him/her. To write with ink is a sign of creativity and increased mental awareness. Colours of ink are also important here as a clue to the interpretation. To see a person writing a letter means that you will soon receive important news.

INQUISITION: To be brought before such an authority is a sign of deep worries, guilt complexes and emotional trauma. To belong to an inquisition underlies a negative streak bordering on the sadistic, that if not quickly checked within the holder will eventually result in self-destructive or self-defeating tendencies. Theocratic fanaticism out of control is also a warning from the gods to pay attention to our physical necessities. Man cannot survive on the spirit alone and only a raving fool thinks otherwise. Pious monotheistic doctrines have long held the world and the physical plane to be evil. "Satan's kingdom!" as fervent zealots so often call it. The same credo also proclaims that only the spiritual level of existence stands to be holy/sacred. Paganism however regards all levels to be sacred. "As above so below!" All planes are different yet essential aspects of divine law. The Inquisition would of course have regarded these comments as being a punishable heresy against God! This would no doubt have quickly resulted in the author's arrest, trial and execution. Fundamentalism always seeks to censor, silence or eventually slaughter its critics in the name of doing good or/and confronting evil. Because of the above this sign is also a warning to be tolerant towards other peoples' beliefs and opinions even when they may initially seem weird, unorthodox, or simply incomprehensible. The Christian Inquisition murdered millions of innocent victims for being different, refusing to conform or simply for being in the wrong place at the wrong time. Unfortunately, the same mindset that led to the foundation stone of this dangerous fundamentalist authority is still very much alive in the depths of human consciousness today. Many well financed and respected religious organisations and charities spend vast amounts of donations on anti-Pagan propaganda each year. This is of course especially true at Halloween when the pragmatic, zealot machine goes into overdrive. These odious factions seek to persuade Joe Public that Pagans/occultists are at best mistaken and at worst evil. This is not simply the author's opinion it is provable fact, gained from years of monitoring the fundamentalist campaign to disenfranchise all religious minorities (especially Pagans) in society. Anyone doubting this truth must heed the following. Several Pagan organisations have previously met great difficulties as charities because the authorities don't consider them to be genuine cases for charitable status. Only monotheistic groups can apparently claim help in this instance. Discrimination against Paganism runs deep in all quarters of society. Ironically, hundreds of belligerent Christian charities continue to be granted charitable status even though they are openly anti-Pagan/occultist in nature. Some are fanatically opposed to every other faith in the world that they see as being satanically inspired. Incredibly, they still qualify for charitable status. This regrettable situation is hardly the sign of a fair, democratic society. The fundamentalists manipulate the tabloid press and work hard to expurgate and even ban traditional Halloween festive fun with many successes. This they do by presenting the authorities (especially schools and places associated with children) with disingenuous propaganda concerning this lovely old native, Celtic festival of summer's end. Instead of the indigenous celebration of Halloween, the fundamentalists suggest (often insist) that the feast be rejected in favour of a Christian alternative celebration. Now I ask you dear reader, how would Christians react if Pagans demanded that their festivals be banned then Paganised? How would Christians take it if

Pagans insisted that carol singing be outlawed as a danger to society, because some teenage delinquents had been terrorising senior citizens by pretending to be genuine vocalists? Naturally, Christians would be appalled at this ludicrous suggestion, yet incidents involving carol singing and crime have in fact recently occurred. In the author's hometown, an old man was reported in the local media as being a victim of riotous, exploitative teenage carol singers. The point I highlight here is that regardless of what celebration takes place, there will always be a batch of fools ready to spoil it for everyone else. Misleading literature of a grossly offensive nature against unorthodox adherents of ancient faiths fills libraries and bookshops everywhere. Sadly, evangelically inspired prejudice is now big business, raking in massive sums of money worldwide every day. This sad situation does nothing to create harmony/balance in what is supposed to be a democratic multi-faith society. The dark side of human nature where evil poses as good never resides far under the surface of human insecurities. When one powerful religion seeks to outlaw smaller ones, we simply end up with the inherent dangers of religious absolutism, encapsulated fully within the sign of the horrendous, all-consuming Inquisition. The inquisition sign warns in no uncertain terms to guard against becoming too pious in one's opinions against other members of humanity. Be tolerant! If we ignore this warning, then we assist in the behaviour of zealotry and deny our species the opportunity to grow in spiritual awareness. We are all individuals; what is right for one may be wrong for another. Life can never be ordered by any so-called holy writ for without the grace of individuality we simply become ant-like automatons fearing to act or even think for ourselves. Beware the sign of the Inquisition for it tells us more about ourselves then we often care to know!

IRON: Iron is weight, so weight represents extra luggage that one can well do without. This is especially so in the

73

hypothetical sense thus it may depict anxieties in the viewer. Iron is connected to protection. Our early ancestors must have felt a lot better with a strong iron lance at their side as opposed to the older, more breakable stone implement. Iron was power and the sign of prestige and defence. If ever there was an emblem for control over sinister force, then this must be it. The aboriginal people of these isles would have regarded iron with a certain amount of trepidation and unease as it was largely the possession of the invading, technically superior Celtic tribes. It represented a new and strange science to some and yet strength and victory to others. Iron is fashioned out of the elements of Mother Earth, so it has attributes with accordance therein. Iron can earth or redirect energy and because of this it has always had a place in the realms of magickal workings. The horseshoe is fashioned from iron so we can hereby observe iron's link to luck and good fortune.

IVY: This sombre green plant has an exceptionally long pedigree in the halls of myth and magick. Priests of the god of rebirth (Attis) wore ivy leaf tattoos upon their bodies. It was eaten during rites of Bacchus to inspire and adherents into greater intimacy with the god. Ivy crowns were worn by the ancients to prevent excess intoxication and they were particularly valued by poets. Osiris, that great Egyptian deity also held ivy as his sacred plant. Ivy also has associations with Thalia (the Muse of comedy.) Used externally, the leaves have a reputation for helping to cure sunburn. The plant is a very hardy evergreen and quick to colonise old cottages, thus it suggests survival against hard odds and qualities of resurrection. Ivy turns man-made ugliness into natural beauty. To see this plant in vision is a sign of longevity and endurance. It can however also be a symbol of sadness, deterioration, melancholy and unrequited love.

JAWS: The terrifying cinematic image of the man-eating Great White Shark is now well implanted into popular contemporary human consciousness. Jaws of savage beasts in vision have always been a powerful symbol of danger/strength. Because jaws tear meat they also connect with feelings about revenge and sometimes even justice. Early man, after escaping the unwanted attention of a wild bear or lion would certainly have had more than a few nightmares about gnashing jaws! Today, the sign of jaws also lends itself to associations with libel, slander, and all types of malicious gossip. Loose mouths are always a danger to freethinkers.

JEWEL: A jewel in vision and dreams is frequently emblematic of increasing wealth and prosperity yet not always in a materialistic sense. Colour of gems and precious stones is also most relevant to the interpretation of the image. The following brief list of ancient divination properties of stones/mineral/metals may be of some assistance to seekers.

ADULARIA. Has calming effect on the mental faculties.
AMAZONITE. Good for healing and wealth attracting.
AMBER. Gives protection and help with health problems.
AMETHYST. For tranquillity and aids against intoxication.
APATITE. To absorb bad vibrations and stop gossip.
AQUAMARINE. Peace and meditation with increased health.
AVENTURINE. For good fortune and success.
AZURITE. Mental faculty and meditations.
BLACK-AGATE. Absorbs negativity and increases strength.
BERYL. Beneficial for the liver and general health.
CALCITE. Soothing and calming properties.
CARNELIAN. Blood purifier and good for new vitality.
CHALCEDONY. Generally, for health and vitality.
CHRYSOCOLLA. Remembrance and loyalty.
CHRYSOLITE. Protection, wealth, and happiness.
CITRINE. Health and clear thinking.
COAL. Continuity, protection, and good luck.
COPPER. For love and protection against illness.
CORAL. For love attraction and magickal workings.
DIAMOND. Clarity of the logical mind and inspiration.

DIORITE. For atonement to the earth's cycles.
EMERALD. Happiness, eye disorders and long life.
FLINT. To protect, inspire and strengthen.
FOSSIL ROCK. Astral travel, lucid dreams, the imagination.
GARNET. For power, strength, energy, and satisfaction.
GOLD. Attraction of Solar energy and wealth.
GRANITE. Earthing negative energy and helping the mind.
GYPSUM. Happiness and relief from stress.
HIDDENITE. For awareness and knowledge of the unknown.
IRON. For protection and redirection of force.
JADE. Helps visualisation and the imagination.
JASPER. Spiritual awareness and the psychic process.
KYANITE. Calming and aids with concentration.
LAPIS LAZULI. Improves intellect and spiritual awareness.
LIMESTONE. Improves appreciation of self and natural world.
MARBLE. Attracts peace and tranquillity.
MOLYBDENITE. For help with mental stress and illness.
MOONSTONE. Psychic ability and spiritual strength.
NICCOLITE. Friendships, love, and fertility.
ONYX. Mental awareness and clarity.
OPAL. Inspires confidence and protection of the ego.
PEARL. Quells aggression and calms the worried mind.
PISOLITE. Attracts affection from opposite sex.
PLATINUM. Psychic protection and strength.
PYRITE. Solar divinations and awareness of self.
QUARTZ. Inspiration, spiritual awareness, and energy.
RUBY. For passion and to invigorate the libido.
SAPPHIRE. Improves intellect and deflects negativity.
SERPENTINE. Increased success and healing associations.
SILVER. Imagination, mystery and the hidden.
SLATE. For remembrance and calmness.
SODALITE. Promotes youth and inner visions.
TIGER'S EYE. For protective and wealth attracting charms.
TIN. Deflects deceit and falsehoods.
TOPAZ. Calms and guards the wearer.
TOURMALINE. Improves sensitivity and energy.
TURQUOISE. Tranquillity, success, and intuition.

URANINITE. Strongly radioactive, beware!
VESUVIANITE. Friendship, happiness, and social affairs.
WOLFRAMITE. Strength and longevity.
ZIRCON. Clarity of mind and inspiration.

JOURNEY: For a depressed person to dream of a fond journey denotes the desire for happiness. For the rich and affluent man/woman to see a trip into dark foreboding places suggests underlying guilt and subconscious worries about possible failure in the world of business. Putting all of one's eggs in the same basket is a mistake and this dream/vision spells out this fact quite clearly.

JUDGE: A symbol of impending justice and final judgement concerning a pressing issue in life. The judge stands for power that cannot be resisted and ultimate authority. Your past actions are soon to be used against you in either a positive or negative manner. You are the cause of the Judge's sentence upon your previous good or bad activities so you can only blame yourself if his finger points at you in a critical fashion. The judge is the hand of karmic justice working towards you. If you are guilty then you must ride the wind like a dragon, accept your fate and learn from your past foolish errors. Every action has its final price!

KALEIDOSCOPE: Abstract events with little concrete foundation. Life for you needs to slow down a touch or else you may miss a lot of excellent opportunities. Do yourself a favour, take a break and relax for a while. Your imagination may be getting carried away with itself.

KEY: The symbol of Janus, great god of doorways and new beginnings. A key unlocks a door and the door in this instance may relate to avenues of forthcoming events either good or bad. See the key herein as a herald of change and exciting new opportunities to come soon. Freedom and liberation from an oppressive situation are also strongly indicated by this powerful symbol. The Egyptian anserated cross (Ankh) is the hieroglyph for the key to life and living. Its key-like structure represents an initiation into spiritual grace and wisdom. It may show us that we stand at an important crossroads in our life quest.

KILLING: To make a killing is a sign of repressed, negative feelings against someone or something in your life. To be killed in a dream marks a desire to escape a troubling situation that seems temporarily out of your control. Death is not a final thing but a mere change of direction, a way to leave the past to start a new life. A worrying future operation, driving test, or job interview may trigger a series of nightmares associated with this dark topic.

KITE: Flying a kite into the wild blue yonder is a sign of freedom and hope. It is also connected with the realms of childhood and days of liberation and innocence. If the kite breaks away into the sky, expect a swift resolution to an important problem soon.

KNOTS: In magickal workings knots are storage receptacles for concentrated energy. They lock in force that would otherwise escape. They are traps then for whatever we wish to put into them. On dream levels they may depict life problems that cannot seem to be mastered. With wisdom there will be a sure solution. It's just a matter of interpreting it and untying the knot. Try hard, be sincere in your manner and the gods will always show you the right direction to take.

LADDER: Advancement or retreat is the message given by this sign. Think of the simple game children play, snakes and ladders. Here we have the perfect encapsulation of progress or/and withdrawal that is concisely marked in emblematic fashion, depicting life events and their effect upon our being. To put it simply, see this sign as a statement of your life and how well or badly it's progressing. Often a warning of a fall in social standing. High time to assess one's current situation. To walk under a ladder is considered bad luck in popular superstition. This may be because a leaning ladder forms a triangle, which is the old elemental sign of fire. Walking into such a sign can then be said to invite the destructive quality of this element into one's life. Of course, witches and occultists often work with fire element just as they do with all the other elements too. With the correct knowledge and preparation all elemental work is safe and beneficial, however fire element must never be treated lightly (for obvious reasons.) Christians used to say that one offended the Holy Trinity by thus strolling under the three-pointed image of an angled ladder. However, in the light of the former, this belief will be seen to be adopted from a much older heathen folklore.

LAKE: A lake is a special place of hidden mystery. Even when dead calm, a beautiful lake exudes a sense of brooding power and majesty. It links intimately with our emotions and lovers are naturally drawn to the timeless allure of water. The sick and low of spirit will also benefit greatly from being close to gentle waters of a lake. Negativity is slowly but surely banished here. This is not just a faddy New Age belief but a concrete fact that must be experienced to be fully understood. In dreams, the action of the lake (either calm or tempestuous) represents the highs and lows of the emotions and their resultant, associated, impressions surrounding our life cycle.

LAMP: To see a lamp in the darkness is a sign of hope. It is also a symbol of spiritual awakening deep within the viewer. In the Tarot the image of the Hermit carrying his lamp shows us that the lonely path can lead to illumination. Away from the crowd and the common herd instincts of man there is the promise of mystical grace and wisdom. The lamp then may be seen as an offer towards a spiritual quest from the old gods themselves. Are you courageous enough to accept this sacred challenge and evolve from your current mundane existence? The final choice must rest with you and you alone!

LAWYER: Possible guilt complexes rising to the surface of one's consciousness. Something long forgotten from the past coming back to haunt the viewer. This is a symbol of legal authority and the deep mind's way of gaining the mundane mind's attention over a pressing matter of some importance. The prudent are wise to investigate this sign and put matters to right. Also, a warning of criticism, especially in the workplace.

LETTERS: Quite a complex symbol this one. Letters depict communication as the image suggests. Good letters containing fine news herald just that. Letters that cause upset denote mishaps and possible loses in terms of friendships/money/business or love. Anonymous letters warn of deceit and skulduggery, launched against the seeker by an unknown cowardly assailant. Letters from old friends tell one that they are thinking about you and may soon make contact, either by mail or otherwise.

LIGHTNING: The physical manifestation of divine light that can destroy and create life. Since time immemorial man has held this symbol in great awe. The druidic priests of the Celts held sacred any oak that was touched (struck) by the gods with lightning. To the Celtic races the god of lightning was Taranis (or possibly Sucellos) to the Romans he was Jupiter-Fulgar, whilst the Etruscans knew him simply as Tin. To see lightning in dreams heralds important changes in one's life. It also depicts an initiation from one state of being to another. When the divine light of the old gods impinges upon one's soul, see it as a blessing of good things to come after hardships have been conquered.

LOVE: Contentment/affection/happiness/friendships and of course beautiful romances are all foretold with this vision. Your life is (or soon shall be) satisfying and wholesome. Venus will enter your life and make everything seen perfect if you open your arms to her blessings. Don't however become too complaisant as although love is essential to a full life it is

80

but only one aspect. Balance in all things is the key to true happiness. Without love on all levels of existence perversion can easily set in. This is particularly true on the physical plane when the lack of bodily attention/affection leads to sexual obsession. Manufactured taboos relating to sexuality (especially in this western culture) have resulted in a tarnished view of the beautiful human physical form. The very disconcerting rise in Christian clergy abuse of innocent minors over the last few years gives evidence of sexual abstinence (i.e., celibacy) turning into a grossly offensive form of twisted evil deviation. Leading clerics have publicly apologised for this terrible situation on numerous occasions but simply saying "sorry" will not change the taboo or properly address this ongoing problem! This odious affair is not confined to any one grouping and exists in all Xtian denominations. The sad lack of love is one of the largest causes of crime today in our society, which usually starts at early age. In the name of the Goddess, it is our duty as citizens of Planet Earth to spread love wherever and whenever we can!

MAGNET: A path of attraction is calling you from your normal interests. This may relate to a physical attraction of an admirer or an offer of wealth and success from a business associate. Care is needed here as the alluring pull of these charms may have hidden qualities yet unknown. When a body is drawn into the orbit of another the former may eventually find it impossible to escape!

MARCH: To be included in a military march, against one's will, is a sign of oppression and the desire for self-liberation. To partake in one as a volunteer marks the wish for power and the attention of others. The march is in effect the viewer's willpower enforcing itself upon what it egotistically sees as lesser mortals.

MASK: To wear a mask is to conceal an aspect of yourself, which you wish to hide. Subconsciously, the mask depicts mystery, deceit, danger, and licentious affairs. Fear is also relevant, as the mask stops one's true nature from being analysed by others. What we cannot see we fear for there is no greater dread than that which belongs to the awful dark realms of the unknown. Contemporary masked heroic comic strip figures like Batman and Spiderman, et al, have ensured that the mask is also a symbol of unexpected assistance when most needed. Older legendary figures of defiance such as Robin Hood and Zorro also join this lofty category. Mankind will always love a dashing masked hero or villain because they represent a braver side of us that usually remains suppressed/untested, deep within the subconscious mind.

MEDAL: The wish for glory and recognition for services rendered from friends and colleagues. The desire to be noticed and taken into consideration. The ego wanting to draw our mundane attention towards greater feats of conquests. Old tatty medals are a sign of disappointment and sadness, yet also at times represent heritage.

MINEFIELD: Obstacles in life that pose an immediate threat to the viewer. These obstacles may not yet be recognised but they could be threatening one from any direction. The fear of any form of movement and change that may not be beneficial. Beware of gossip and slanderous accusations both from others and by yourself.

MIRROR: A symbol sacred to the Moon Goddess and the reflective element of water. Magickal mirrors have been used throughout the ages in similar fashion to the crystal ball, thus mirrors link with aspects of divination and the magickal arts. Any reflective image can soothe the chattering mind and allow the deeper levels to conjoin with the hidden world. In dreams and vision, mirrors depict analytical periods in life when we need to stand back and take a long hard look at events occurring. Also, an image that tells up to examine our own actions with care! Mirrors are also doorways to greater spiritual awareness. Let the Lunar Goddess show you the lightened path with this mysterious image.

MOON: Dreams of the Moon belong to the spiritual realm. They also mark the feminine side of divinity i.e., the Lunar Goddess. In a man's dream the Moon represents the feminine aspect of his nature and the intuitive, nourishing, and formative part of himself that often lies suppressed. To a woman the Moon in vision/dreams stands for her fulfilment in life and the fertilising aspect within. The lunar orb links with the menstrual cycle lasting one month (originally moonth) and the waxing/full and waning aspects of the Moon correspond with the feminine fertility period. Whereas the solar orb depicts the harsh, visual light of day and the conscious mind, the Moon is very much the reverse image i.e., the unknown countenance of night, magick, and the subconscious mindset.

MOUNTAIN: Pleasant climbs up gentle inclines denote success in any future enterprise. Hard dangerous climbs up wet slippery mountains foretell of failure and accidents ahead. Take time to examine your situation and you might be able to save yourself a great deal of disappointment. The mountain is a challenge in one form or another. Spiritually, it depicts the heavens/sky (God) conjoining with the earth (Goddess) to bring forth life and fruitful abundance.

MUSEUM: A symbol of childhood and nostalgia. Evident visual history of the museum is your own personal heritage that you have created for yourself. If the images in the scene are good, then your background is quite sound. However, if you are disturbed by the exhibits then some part of your past has resurfaced to plague you. The answer to one's problem will be there somewhere. You must therefore analyse the symbolic messages that the gods are sending to you through the vehicle of your subconscious mind!

NAVY: War ships on a steady course are emblematic of victory over strong adversaries and problems. They also stand for regaining health after illness. To see a navy sink is a sign of overdoing things and mental strain. Maybe it's time for a holiday away from the hustle and bustle of workday affairs.

NET: Entrapment, captivation, and evangelisation. Although somewhat ambiguous, all these concepts and more figure strongly within the scope of this sign. To net something or be netted means that one has set a plan in motion or is frustrated by disappointments or delays, respectively. The net also links with death and the watery realm. Gladiators armed with sword and shield once faced the grave danger of the Retiarius (fighter armed with trident and net.) The depths of the sea remind us of the net used to haul in Neptune's harvest. The net is also, like a spider's web, the instrument which seizes the unwary traveller and denies them access to their true path. I would suggest that one should view this symbol with much respect, for it may be a timely warning from the gods that all is not well in your life at present.

Numbers

Numbers are like letters because they are in fact visualised concepts/ideas concisely represented in understandable symbolic form. The following list may be helpful to seekers.

ONE: The illuminating Sun and daylight; the centre, initiation or start of all things. One is the logical conscious mind and the dawn of spirituality in the human being.

TWO: Two is duality and the balance displayed by male and female/God and Goddess principles. Three cannot be brought to light without one and two.

THREE: The result of growth from the foundation blocks of duality. It is the Holy Trinity expressed in Pagan lunar terms as waxing, full and waning moon or alternatively, maiden, mother, and crone. The sacred triad of Rome and the universal Triple Goddess in all her glory. Also depicts the stressful (yet creative) conflict arising from the actual clashing together of the first two.

FOUR: The four corners of a square, which link to the earth element and the four cardinal points of the compass conjoining with seasonal cycles of nature. Also, the number of protections.

FIVE: The four elements plus spirit that penetrates all, as such it is the pentagram sacred to the witches' altar. Five stands for the main senses of man, which allow him to experience existence to the full. Five is also the day and note of Venus, thus it depicts love, fertility, and happiness.

SIX: This represents consolidation and unification through the joining of two three pointed triangles that in turn create a six-pointed star. Six is the hidden sense that allows one to access the world of mystery, divination and magick.

SEVEN: Seven links to the sum of days of the week and the deities/planetary cycles corresponding therein. It is thus a symbol of perfect completion through endurance, hardship and sometimes even pain.

EIGHT: A sign that represents the equalisation of opposing agents. The serpents rampant on the Caduceus of Hermes fight and strain against each other to create eventual harmony, finally accomplished in the winding image of the figure eight. It is also a life sign through the cellular -like mating of two creative twisting circles.

NINE: The triple strength of the triumvirate Goddess is a symbol of great power and truth. Today, because of its association with emergency services i.e., 999, this sign represents speedy assistance in popular human consciousness. Ancient man also needed frequent help and the Goddess obviously once fulfilled the spiritual necessity for an emergency psychic helpline in times of greatest danger.

TEN: The pentacle doubled is another power sign. The actual duplication of the five-pointed star leads us to a blatant mirror image that results in reflective lunar qualities. Ten, with its nostalgic reflection, brings us back again to the unifying aspects of one. It is a symbol to some of return, reincarnation, and a new state of being.

NUNS: Because of the aspect of alienation from normal society, dreams and visions of nuns foretell of subconscious feelings of solitude/widowhood/grief/taboo/desires and illicit love affairs. Also denotes religiously indoctrinated sexual guilt and revulsion towards natural human erotic relationships, via unhealthy fanaticism bordering on the completely insane. Rampant and unhealthy female authority god mad, deluded, and suffering from a destructive fear of the opposite sex and well as low self-esteem. In a man's dream, nuns may represent frigidity, loneliness, and impotence. In a woman's dream they are symbolic of scapegoatism, by substituting real earthy desires for illusory friends. The deeply sinister aspect of this symbol has found its way into modern horror movies for good reason, although directors may not even realise this fact.

NURSE: If a nurse is visiting you in vision, then take care of your health for this is a strong sign that all is not well. The nurse is also a desire for attention and relief from the humdrum problems of daily life. She or he stands as a mediator between you and the doctor, thus the nurse is a barrier or hurdle between oneself and the fear of the surgeon's knife. In this context, the nurse becomes a defender protecting you from the terrors of the unknown.

See the nurse then as a guardian albeit, one who reminds us of those dark things residing deep within ourselves, which we would often rather not face. The common populace frequently calls nurses angels. Quite possibly there is a higher meaning/truth at work here that does link the caring, mundane to the higher bastions of existence.

NYMPHS: A nymph is a wild aspect of divinity, a nature spirit inhabiting streams and woodlands. To see one in dream/vision is a sign of passion, love and sexuality. The love may not be for another human but for nature and life itself. Of course, the know all sceptic always scoffs at the mention of such things. To this I say, the consciousness is more perceptive in some than in others. To think that we are the only beings in this vast universe with spirituality is really a type of intellectual fascism. The intuition, consciousness and perception are (like the eyes) stronger in some individuals than in others. Just because some people fail to perceive hidden creatures of spirit such as elementals, nymphs, dryads, etc., does not mean that they do not exist. Those depressing sceptics who have never opened their cobweb-encrusted minds and souls to the wonders of the incredible hidden world, may never hope to understand the magnificence of the old gods and the awesome, unseen, greater natural forces that impinge upon us each day. The danger to profaners of ignoring the hidden dimension or even ridiculing it simply results in a loss only to themselves. By crass ego-related actions they put the brake firmly on their own spiritual evolution and self-impose limitations, which eventually create nothing more than gross negativity and lack of balance. Man will always attack that which he does not understand. Wise occultists realise this fact and make necessary allowances for it, with a smile.

OIL: Black crude is a sign of wealth, yet it also reminds us of pollution and catastrophe within nature. Oil, in the sense of oils for beauty and health, are signs of contact. In magick, oil transports the essence of the aura to a given object or person.

In aromatherapy, oil draws on the divergent essences of plants, which have in turn condensed sun energy in their own special way to grant one health giving favours. Oil in cookery is a sign of worldly desire and the need for attention. Oil is thus a sign of transportation of one element into another. The type of oil seen is the type of blessing or threat to be expected, albeit in symbolic fashion. An open mind and the need for discernment are the keys to understanding such images in dream and vision.

ONIONS: These have an old reputation for being good to combat colds and chill. Magickally, they are used for banishing negativity and to promote courage as they come under the influence of Mars, a Roman god of war. To dream of onions is to realise that there is a threat to one's well-being close at hand. Identify it and you will be victorious.

ORANGES: Sacred to the Sun god. Oranges are a good sign of riches and plenty. Used magickly to boost the aura and purify, they are an excellent image to aid in visualisation. Generally, a symbol of satisfaction, wealth and success.

PALACE: To see yourself in a plush palace full of riches is a sign of increasing fortune. A ramshackle palace, which is in a state of decay, is symbolic of lost opportunities and sad events troubling the viewer.

PANCAKE: An economical or even overtly thrifty situation is set to affect the viewer if pancakes are seen in vision. Tossing pancakes into the air is however comparable with happiness and the chance for liberation from life worries and stress.

PANTOMIME: The surrealism embracing this comic vision foretells the viewer that life is not always as it seems. Mistrust and deceit are waiting around the corner for the unwary. The bizarre characters in the pantomime are often shadows of real individuals, who we know only too well.

Their actions in the scene foretell of their intentions to us, which we sometimes would rather not know about.

PATH: Much depends on the sort of path encountered. To approach a lonely crossroads portends of important decisions ahead. To see a quiet straight pathway tells us that life is presently set to be calm and uneventful. A twisting path is a sign of pleasure and fun times ahead, whereas a steep uphill path warns of hardship and troubles to come.

PEA: Symbolic with good fortune, wealthy dealings and help from others. Their colour links with the good earth and this marks the worldly bounty that they promise. Especially a good sign for farmers, gardeners, and anyone else connected with horticulture.

PENCIL: To write with one indicates the desire to communicate with others, even so much as to be a serious demand for attention. To see others writing with pencils displays a subconscious wish to find out a secret. It can also represent a need to be noticed with affection.

PERFUME: Pleasant aromas in dream and vision are not uncommon. Perfume is a sign of romance, sexuality, and unadulterated lust. There is a certain note of whirlwind affairs and glamour involved here too, which may warn of the breakup of present stable relationships.

PIER: This image stretches deep into the sea and because water is often analogous with the subconscious, the pier becomes a trip into the unknown regions of the mind and beyond. To stand firmly upon a solid pier is emblematic of strong mental ability and the desire to be triumphant. To see a pier sinking into the sea is a warning that one must change course in life soon, or else trouble will occur!

PIPE: A length of pipe (as used in industry) is without doubt a symbol that contains phallic connotations. However, the smoking pipe is associated with wisdom, (the peace pipe) advice and contentment.

PIRATE: Often given as a sign of deceit, theft, and false hopes. This may be so in most cases; however, the pirate can also be emblematic of freedom, bravado, and liberation from oppressive forces. The pirate's link to the (subconscious) sea suggests connections to a disturbed mindset, which requires addressing rather quickly.

POISON: To be poisoned in dreams denotes mistrust from others working clandestinely against your best interests. To be the poisoner marks the desire to eradicate life's problems that seem to be overwhelming you. Also, a sign of revenge against what the mind regards as personal injustice.

POPE: Symbol of religious bondage and total authority. Also, because of infamous historical transgressions, a mark of cruelty and injustice against minorities. This latter distinction is today further strengthened when we consider previous Vatican statements against Paganism that sought to place the blame for the Nazi Holocaust on the heads on Pagans. This ludicrous Christian blood libel was largely accepted without question by the gullible masses as fact, thus the persecution of a religious minority continues unabated. The Pope, as the leading light in this wholesale vilification of a spiritual community, must carry the responsibility on all levels including those met in dream and vision!

POSTMAN: A sign of unexpected news arriving in your life, as the image blatantly suggests. Also, anxiety and indecision are possible connections herein.

PRIEST: Guilt, oppression, authority, hardship, misery, and serfdom are all marked by this sign. Contrary to popular belief, priesthoods of any type have always been instigated to stop the populace from gaining direct links to divinity. They act as a self-appointed mediator between the trusting adherent and his chosen god. This well-tested old mind control system may not be realised on a conscious level, yet the shrewd subconscious mind picks it up and converts it into oppressive images. Can 'you' see through the confusion of the priestly middleman image? If you can't, then it just goes to show how well a priesthood has manipulated you and has managed to indoctrinate you into blind compliance.

PYRAMID: This ancient icon has associations with heat and fire. Not only the fire of hot places like Egypt, where these vast structures are found, but the fire of the human spirit. See them as signs in vision of enlightenment and wisdom for their Pagan heritage holds many secrets yet still undiscovered by contemporary man.

QUICKSAND: A rather negative symbol of misfortune and events that the conscious mind wishes to hush-up! It also marks the desire to escape responsibilities, which one does not view with happy anticipation.

RAFT: To sail away in a raft from a place of captivity denotes the wish for liberation. To sail a raft into stormy waters foretells of unhappy events ahead (especially in personal relationships.)

RAILWAY: A sign of communication and travel to far places. These places may however not be of the physical world; thus, they frequently represent ambitions which one is set to achieve in life. The state of the track and vehicles therein will give evidence to this image's positive or negative meaning.

RAINBOW: Symbolic of happy events and great success. The gold at the end of the rainbow (as in the old saying) doubtless refers to spiritual enlightenment. Expect to gain greater awareness after seeing this lovely sign.

RAKE: Hard work and endurance are suggested here. A broken rake is a warning though of misfortune in the workplace.

RHUBARB: Slightly comical connections reside in this symbol, largely because of vulgar pantomime associations. View it as a symbol of fast growth in business/relationships tempered with possible mishaps caused by lack of attention to detail.

RINGS: Rings are of course complete circles, consequently holding all the associations therein with these symbols. Because rings are habitually made from precious stones and gold they stand for wealth and prosperity. Furthermore, they denote love, friendships, and lasting memories, albeit sometimes marked by nostalgic sadness. Their condition (dull or shiny) in dreams gives us a clue as to their applicable meaning.

RIVER: Rivers are in a fashion the veins of Mother Earth. They denote the transposition of energy from one place to another. They remind us that life is never static but always moving, ergo they represent our emotions that change on a constant basis from good to bad and vice versa. Rivers also link with powerful healing for there is no finer a place to be than the water's edge when illness threatens.

ROOF: "Shout it from the roof-tops!" This saying is linked to celebration and happiness. Being so excited that one must yell out loud is a sign of victory and liberation from harsh oppression. Being on a roof in dreams is to gain advancement and prestige over other mortals. However, to fly from a high roof may denote astral travel (actual or wished for.) Falling from such lofty places is a warning of possible impending disaster. Realise and combat your fears instead of suppressing them.

SAND: Multi-complex sign this one. On one hand it marks the fear of loss and poverty, however it may also represent the desire for holidays, fun, and love. If accompanied by feelings of thirst, then wake up and take a drink! Simple health warning from the mind to eat less salt with your food.

SCEPTRE: A regal sign of good fortune and prosperity. Expect to achieve your ambitions soon. Also, a symbol of overseeing a situation that other people fear.

SCYTHE: The instrument of the (Grim) Reaper and as such, a symbol of death and removal. This need not be an image to fear because the death aspect may be more connected with death of a situation, rather than oneself or other persons. The scythe of the reaper must remove the old to bring in the new. This is the prime law of the universe, and we must realise its inherent wisdom. See it primarily as a warning to modify your ways and improve your present situation.

SKELETON: Taking away the vital life materials from a body and leaving it exposed as nothing more than white bones betokens injustice, offence and ailments directed toward the viewer. A pertinent warning to take good care. Also, a sign of banishment or being deprived of previous accolades.

SMOKE: We of course cannot see through thick smoke thus to the subconscious mind it holds secrets and intrigue. It is the hidden world just beyond the physical that contains fear yet at the same time fascination. Smoke also connects to fire element and human emotion therein. Because of this latter aspect, see it as a possible warning to beware of deceit in romantic areas of your life. What lies past/behind the smoke (emotional state) may not be good for you. Additionally, it may denote news from afar, as in the Native American Indian smoke signal system.

SOLDIER: As the image would suggest, marching soldiers are a sign of order and established logical thinking. To be attacked by soldiers is a warning not to run before you can walk, or in other words, do not take on too many commitments, which may cramp your style and weigh you down. Soldiers that are wounded are a sign of misfortune, hardship and unfulfilled ambitions.

STAIRS: To travel downstairs is symbolic of disappointment, fears, and unhappy events. To go up stairways gives evidence of social improvement and successful outcomes to pressing problems.

STEEPLE: This image is intricately linked to feeling of apprehension and misfortune. Like the Tower card in the Tarot deck, it can frequently be an omen of destructive tendencies. This may not be as adverse as would first seem to be the case. The destruction of one establishment makes way for the new and often better to come. It must be said that the phallic-shaped steeple is also representative with masculine fecundity and associated aspects hence connected.

SUN: The sign of greatest wealth and abundance, especially if viewed at its midday zenith. The rising red sun is the promise of future aspirations that may not have just yet matured into fulfilment. The dying sun that slowly sets, hissing into the wild blue ocean represents romantic nostalgia. It is the logical, clear, mindset as opposed to the instinctive/intuitive lunar realm. Without the life-giving solar orb, we are nothing and our deepest selves know this truth well. See it as a concomitant part of our ancient connection to nature and what lies beyond the mysteries of life, death, and resurrection.

SWORD: If shining and proper, a noble emblem of honour, courage, and trust. If broken and rusty, a symbol of deceit, treachery, and cowardice. For more information on this image kindly study the previous listing on 'cards'.

TABLE: Early image which usually connects with feelings of family and friends. The focal point of domestic life and decisions taken therein. The (good or bad) state of the table indicates the current situation at home or what is soon to manifest herein.

TATTOO: This sign marks the deep desire to be special/to be noticed (loved) by others, hence it can be symbolic of insecurity and anxiety in social/romantic circles. Also connects with the exotic and strange. Anything which diverts from the norm or institutionally acceptable.

TEETH: this symbol forms an important link to all that is essential for survival on planet earth. Teeth allow us to eat, fight and communicate feelings with other beings. Because of this they are in dreams signs of self-expression and the ego. To see teeth that fall out denotes illness and sorrow. To see white, sparkling teeth is symbolic of romance and happiness. Teeth that rip and tear are a warning of enemies that wish to destroy one's reputation with slander and malice.

THORN: Under the green mantle of nature's beauty lies a darker, more uncomfortable reality. The lovely rose, the sweet-scented hawthorn, the ubiquitous bramble flower. All these delightful natural creations remind the prudent to be aware, for the sacred natural balance of joy must mingle with pain, on all levels of existence. In layman's terms, see this vision as a 'sharp' warning not to trust everything that appears at first glance to be trustworthy or of elegant allure.

UFO: An unidentified flying object (UFO) in dreams is not uncommon. It may herald new enterprises, or even whirlwind romantic relationships that are on the horizon. Also, the suppressed desire for liberation from humdrum, every day, worldly events. Incidentally, I have written two books about UFO sightings around the world. These works may be accessed through my various links.

UNDERGROUND: Subterranean adventures or journeys in vision are frequently astral tours back into our own individual history. The underground realm is within us and can also relate to deeply hidden emotions, and fears, which come back in dreamtime to haunt us. This is the dwelling place of the unknown and all that is shrouded in dark mystery. Since time immemorial mystics of old have travelled to sinister underground caverns/caves to seek out ancient truths,
which cannot be recorded in logical terms. These truths reside within each of us and must be experienced on a personal intuitive plane to be fully understood. This is one of the prime ambitions of magickal practice for witch or shaman. To make known that which was before wholly undetermined, and thus become a greater being. The fluidic structure of the universe will bend before us, if we allow the energies granted to us by the old gods to flourish!

URN: A link with the past and that which has gone before. Often associated with feelings of funerals and death. Can also relate to work and all that connects therein. May represent a secret that must be explored/discovered before personal evolution can progress.

VEIL: Symbolic of the unknown realm and fears therein. To see another person standing before one shrouded in a veil means that a stranger is near, who cannot yet be trusted. To view oneself veiled denotes a keen desire for intimacy, anonymity, and clandestine meetings. Also, a sign of change and initiation from one level of existence to another. A common example is the veiled bride who leaves the wedding altar to start a vastly different lifestyle.

VOLCANO: The primordial forces of nature in vision remind us that all of man's ambitions stand no chance against the awesome wrath of the gods. Without doubt the volcano is destructive energy yet at the same time it is sexual prowess that creates vital new life. A sound emblem of big changes to come.

WAITER: The embodiment of servitude and aspects associated within. To be waited on in dreams denotes several possibilities. It may be the desire for luxuries that others have achieved. Then again, it may be linked to the need for power. It can be a sign of insecurity and the wish to dominate others. The waiter gives so that we may receive; henceforth he is emblematic of personal sacrifices, which we must sometimes make in life.

WAR: Visions of war denote struggles and hardships to be faced. The realm of Mars is however not one to be always feared. War is like winter, destructive yet it makes way for the new by extinguishing the old, therefore creation continues undiminished. Defeat is as the name suggests emblematic with personal sadness, just as visions of victory herald glad tiding and profit.

WATCH: In the framework of eternity what is time? It is a mindset that we have created to measure the total knowable span of our lives, to try and make sense of the mystery of human consciousness. The watch or clock represents this concept and its deep residing mysticism. The watch is symbolic of passing life (time) and evolution both individual and that on a wider cultural scale. This sign is personal to you and largely resists generalisation, therefore make of it what you will!

WHEEL: Ancient sign of life, continuity, infinity, and fertility. It is a circular image as is the life-giving solar orb. Its link with continuity stems from its constant forward motion. The wheel conjoins symbolically with the circle that has no beginning and no end, hence its link with infinity. These latter aspects are progressive so naturally they in turn have come to signify sexual progress, which is fertility personified. Furthermore, any idea/concept connected with the solar orb must be seen as holding inherent magickal properties of wondrous fertility. For many persons today the wheel is seen at face value as merely another emblem of transport. However, the above gives evidence that this sign contains a much greater wisdom, which exists just under the cloak of the mundane consciousness of the masses.

YACHT: A simple emblem of fair dealings and the desire to escape everyday tediousness. This sign in dreams is a beneficial herald of good things coming your way and ambitions going according to plan. Time to go forth and prosper!

ZOO: Primordial dangers inherent in savage beasts have been tamed, or at least censored, within this place. Because of this the zoo is emblematic of personal fears and anxieties that we have learnt to control. For more on zoo symbology please see the previous section dealing with divergent animal symbols. Feeding the animals at a zoo is to understand our own emotions and thus denotes a certain maturity. If a wild animal escapes, then beware, for this is a sign that illness, gloom, or deceit is at hand! With this image, much depends on the type of animal encountered.

The sign brings us to the end of this guidebook. It must be repeated that this dream guide is for guidance purposes only. The person best qualified to deal with dream/vision interpretation is most always the actual holder of the vision.

It is however my sincere wish that this succinct analysis will help to point seekers in the right direction for greater awareness of self and the wonderous universe beyond.

One last thing...

You now have the opportunity to rate this book and share your thoughts on Amazon, Facebook, Google, and Twitter, etc. If you consider that this volume is worth sharing, please do take a few moments to let your friends know about it.

Many thanks for joining me on this fascinating journey.

Pat Regan

Southport

July 2021

Additional books by Pat Regan

CONFESSIONS OF A TWENTY- FIRST CENTURY BLOGGER

UK Paperback: https://www.amazon.co.uk/dp/1788083644/

US paperback: https://www.amazon.com/dp/1788083644

UK Kindle version: https://www.amazon.co.uk/Confessions-Twenty-First-Century-Blogger-changing-ebook/dp/B083ZR2LQY/

US Kindle version: https://www.amazon.com/Confessions-Twenty-First-Century-Blogger-changing-ebook/dp/B083ZR2LQY/

PAGAN HERITAGE: SPIRITUAL BIRTHRIGHT OF THE BRITISH ISLES

UK Paperback: https://www.amazon.co.uk/Pagan-Heritage-Spiritual-Birthright-British/dp/1541186729/

US paperback: https://www.amazon.com/Pagan-Heritage-Spiritual-Birthright-British/dp/1541186729/

UK Kindle: http://www.amazon.co.uk/Pagan-Heritage-Spiritual-Birthright-British-ebook/dp/B01D27RRDK/

US Kindle: https://www.amazon.com/Pagan-Heritage-Spiritual-Birthright-British-ebook/dp/B01D27RRDK/

UFO: THE SEARCH CONTINUES

UK Paperback: http://www.amazon.co.uk/UFO-Continues-Mr-Pat-Regan/dp/1511569751/

US paperback: http://www.amazon.com/UFO-Continues-Mr-Pat-Regan/dp/1511569751/

UK Kindle: http://www.amazon.co.uk/UFO-Search-Continues-Pat-Regan-ebook/dp/B00VPB54QI/

US Kindle: http://www.amazon.com/UFO-Search-Continues-Pat-Regan-ebook/dp/B00VPB54QI/

THE DEVIL GOD'S BEST FRIEND

US Paperback version: http://www.amazon.com/Devil-Gods-Best-Friend/dp/1493643363/

UK Paperback version: http://www.amazon.co.uk/Devil-Gods-Best-Friend/dp/1493643363/

UK Kindle: https://www.amazon.com/Devil-Gods-Best-Friend-ebook/dp/B00GOH7XEO/

US Kindle: http://www.amazon.com/Devil-Gods-Best-Friend-ebook/dp/B00HRH6LKC/

PETER SWIFT AND THE SECRET OF GENOUNIA

UK version: http://www.amazon.co.uk/Peter-Swift-Secret-Genounia-1/dp/1478336595/ref=sr_1_2?s=books&ie=UTF8&qid=1345541982&sr=1-2

US Version: http://www.amazon.com/Peter-Swift-Secret-Genounia-1/dp/1478336595/

UK Kindle version: http://www.amazon.co.uk/Peter-Swift-Secret-Genounia-ebook/dp/B008QO3F86/

US Kindle version: http://www.amazon.com/Peter-Swift-Secret-Genounia-ebook/dp/B008QO3F86/

FLY FISHING ON WILD BECKS

UK paperback: http://www.amazon.co.uk/dp/1481250000/

US paperback: https://www.amazon.com/Fly-fishing-wild-becks-Regan/dp/1481250000/

UK Kindle version: http://www.amazon.co.uk/Fly-fishing-wild-becks-ebook/dp/B00ANPDQZ8/

US Kindle Version: http://www.amazon.com/Fly-fishing-wild-becks-ebook/dp/B00ANPDQZ8/

UFO: THE SEARCH FOR TRUTH (2012, EXTENDED EDITION)

UK Paperback version: http://www.amazon.co.uk/UFO-Search-Mr-Pat-Regan/dp/1479149128/

US Paperback version: http://www.amazon.com/UFO-Search-Mr-Pat-Regan/dp/1479149128/

UK Kindle: http://www.amazon.co.uk/dp/B00B93A8Z4/

US Kindle: http://www.amazon.com/dp/B00B93A8Z4

THE NEW PAGAN HANDBOOK - REVISED 2017 EDITION

UK Site: https://www.amazon.co.uk/dp/1977861989/

US Site: https://www.amazon.com/dp/1977861989/

US Kindle edition: http://www.amazon.com/dp/B0051BTWNO

UK Kindle edition: https://www.amazon.co.uk/dp/B0051BTWNO

DIRTY POLITICS

UK edition: http://www.amazon.co.uk/dp/1482031248/

US edition: http://www.amazon.com/dp/1482031248/

UK Kindle edition: http://www.amazon.co.uk/Dirty-Politics-ebook/dp/B00B3L7EDQ/

US Kindle edition: http://www.amazon.com/Dirty-Politics-ebook/dp/B00B3L7EDQ/

THE TORCH AND THE SPEAR

US Site: http://www.amazon.com/Torch-Spear-Patrick-Regan/dp/1898307725/

UK Site: http://www.amazon.co.uk/Torch-Spear-Patrick-Regan/dp/1898307725

PAT REGAN ON AMAZON:

http://www.amazon.com/-/e/B002GWKPOQ

PAT ON US TV:

http://www.youtube.com/watch?v=5sETokzBw8Y&feature=player_embedded

http://www.youtube.com/watch?v=HgKYWoNaKaY

http://www.youtube.com/watch?v=9s4YRwi4tFw

AUTHOR SITE 1:
http://patregan.jimdo.com

AUTHOR SITE 2:
http://patregan.wix.com/pat-regan

AUTHOR SITE 3:
http://pat-regan.weebly.com/

AUTHOR BLOG:
http://pat-regan.blogspot.co.uk

FACEBOOK:
https://www.facebook.com/reganclan

PAT REGAN PHOTOGRAPHY:
https://www.picfair.com/users/PatReganphotography